"In this new work, Audrey Lee brings her trademark clarity and precision to the task of demystifying the sometimes opaque world of workplace mediation. She tackles common questions faced by mediators as they work to assess, prepare, and meet parties where they are. In doing so, Lee conveys to readers the same thoughtful, considered expertise that is the hallmark of her Harvard courses."

—Nicole Bryant, Managing Director, Program on Negotiation at Harvard Law School

"*Navigating Conflicts at Work: A Guide to Workplace Mediation* is a thoughtful and practical resource for anyone seeking to strengthen and sustain professional relationships—whether leading complex workplace conversations, managing everyday team dynamics, or approaching conflict through a mediator's lens. Lee blends emotional insight with clear structure, guiding readers through difficult situations with both empathy and strategy. It offers a clear, organized framework for understanding and navigating workplace conflict."

—Charlotte Wager, Chief Talent Officer, Jenner & Block LLP

"I have spent nearly five decades navigating workplace conflict in Australia—as a union official, a company director, a conciliator and arbitrator at the Fair Work Commission (Australia's national workplace relations tribunal), and now as our nation's regulator, the Fair Work Ombudsman. Across all these roles, the most durable and mutually beneficial resolutions have consistently come from applying the core values and techniques of mediation. This book captures those foundational mediation values and techniques. It offers a practical, accessible guide for anyone wanting to understand how early, interestbased mediation can resolve conflict in a constructive and lasting way. I commend it as a valuable resource for anyone navigating workplace disputes or supporting others through them."

—Anna Booth, Australia's Fair Work Ombudsman and past Deputy President, Fair Work Commission

"Audrey Lee delivers a powerful, comprehensive guide that places readers firmly in control of their own workplace conflicts. Blending the best of theory with real-world application, she brings concepts to life through vivid storytelling, relatable examples, and practical, easy-to-follow advice. This isn't just a book you read—it's a toolkit you'll return to again and again."

—Andrea Kupfer Schneider, Professor of Law and Director, Kukin Program for Conflict Resolution, Cardozo School of Law

"Have you ever faced a challenging workplace conflict that seemed impossible to resolve? With over 30 years in public service—as a firefighter, personnel manager, and mediator—I've learned that conflict resolution isn't just a skill; it's a vital service. Having built an in-house workplace mediation program, I also understand the challenges that come with it—particularly navigating misinformation about what mediation is and is not and the absence of practical, reliable resources. This book fills that gap. It equips leaders and mediators alike with a step-by-step approach to resolving conflict while fostering a culture where every voice is heard and respected."

—Gregory Burton, Personnel Officer and Mediation Coordinator, Boston Fire Department

"*Navigating Conflict at Work* is the perfect resource for anyone interested in learning how to approach workplace conflict more productively. Lee marshals her experience across sectors to bring the concepts to life. Using concrete strategies and examples, she deftly responds to the most common questions people ask about using mediation at work. Mediators and parties alike will come away with the information they need to participate in assisted dispute resolution more meaningfully and successfully."

—Rachel Milner Gillers, Associate Professor of the Practice and Director of the Conflict Transformation Lab, Georgetown University

"Long overdue in the catalogue of dispute resolution literature, *Navigating Conflicts at Work* is a masterclass in addressing workplace conflict. Audrey Lee strikes a thoughtful balance between theory and pragmatism while offering essential insights for everyone from organizational leaders to parties entrenched in disputes and those of us tasked with facilitating resolution. A must-read for anyone interested in the complex dynamics of workplace mediation."

—Marcus Stergio, Ombudsperson, Massachusetts Institute of Technology

"'I just want to stick it to [my manager],' a *pro se* complainant once told me, insisting on filing a Charge of Discrimination at the Massachusetts Commission Against Discrimination. Plaintiff clients were often fixated on an offhand comment at work years ago completely unrelated to their legal claims against the employer defendant. In my many years of employment law experience, I have seen litigation matters that could have and/or should have *not been* in the first place. With real life examples and concise insights, Audrey Lee's book is the ultimate user-friendly practical guide for any legal or nonlegal professional navigating workplace conflicts for a chance at not only avoiding litigation but also allowing business continuity and even building stronger relationships. This book presents a clear, structured path on how to mediate workplace conflicts including the *why* behind each step. Every sentence is imbued with Lee's mastery of, deep understanding in, and care for the topic."

—Sujin Han, employment lawyer, former MCAD investigator, trained mediator

"This book is a masterclass for mediators and leaders alike. Audrey's expertise shines through every page, offering a refreshing and highly actionable guide to help anyone navigate this kind of conflict with confidence."

—Seth McNew, mediator and former communications manager at Google

"Throwing your arms up about workplace conflicts? This is the book for you. In *Navigating Conflict at Work*, Audrey Lee, an experienced workplace coach and mediator, takes abstract notions of conflict and negotiation theory and provides nuts and bolts approaches to handling the daily conflicts that any manager can relate to. This book should be on every supervisor's shelf."

—Art Hinshaw, Associate Dean for Experiential Learning and Faculty Director, Lodestar Dispute Resolution Center, Sandra Day O'Connor College of Law, Arizona State University

"Audrey Lee practices what she preaches. *Navigating Conflicts at Work* empowers people to handle workplace conflict with confidence and educates organizational leaders about when and how to introduce external mediators. Effective conflict management fosters healthy, respectful, and productive workplaces. I hope this guide encourages employers across all sectors to utilize and invest in workplace mediation."

—Morgan Glass, Director of Organizational Development, City of Boston

"In *Navigating Conflicts at Work*, Audrey Lee offers valuable practical guidance to mediators, managers, HR officials, and anyone else wrestling with the effort to resolve workplace conflicts. With an accessible and straightforward writing style, she introduces her readers to central concepts in the field of conflict resolution, explains them and then adapts them to the unique and often challenging situations of workplace conflict. Audrey cleverly organizes the bulk of the book around 25 of the most commonly asked questions about workplace mediation and sorts them into the chronological stages of the usual mediation process. She takes on tough questions that may confront the conflict resolvers, such as strong emotions, neutrality, and imbalances of power and answers them honestly and openly, especially for a young and still growing field. She then leaves her readers with an excellent store of tools and resources as well as paths for further learning."

—Brad Honoroff, Mediator, The Mediation Group

"What draws me to this book is how interactive it is. Questions and quizzes that make people think. And after they have reflected on their experience, the book gives them clear directions on next steps. This book draws on the wisdom of years of experience and study and translates it into implementable steps. It is not only approachable but also a powerful tool for bringing peace to the workplace."

—Dr. Clare Fowler, Executive VP of Mediate.com, 2024 International Woman of Peace Award, workplace mediator

"Right from the first chapter, Audrey Lee's debut book draws you in through its accessible style, rich with compelling cases and detailed scenarios stemming from Lee's decades of experience managing workplace conflict. With clear, actionable guidance, Lee masterfully unpacks even the most tangled relationships, all through her deep expertise in mediation and dispute resolution. As an established higher education professional, I found the layered examples highly relatable; yet the guidance Lee offers extends to new and seasoned leaders in any industry who are navigating complex workplace dynamics. Fans of the 'Getting to Yes' approach to negotiation and those seeking real-life solutions for entrenched conflicts will find Lee's insights invaluable. If you want practical strategies that can transform personal and professional relationships and a deeper understanding of unique industry challenges, this book is an absolute must-have."

—Geertrui M. Spaepen, Associate Provost for Operations & Initiatives, The University of Chicago

"*Navigating Conflict at Work* is a practical, highly readable guide that helps in-house lawyers decide whether, when, and how to mediate conflicts in the workplace—even their own. It offers a clear, concise playbook for engaging in effective mediation, tailored to real-world workplace dynamics. In-house counsel who may be called on to 'step' in at various stages of a conflict will find concrete tools, questions, and frameworks they can use right away to resolve workplace conflicts thoughtfully and successfully."

—Jennifer Kobayashi, Associate General Counsel, Aon

Navigating Conflicts at Work

A GUIDE TO WORKPLACE MEDIATION

AUDREY J. LEE

AMERICAN BAR ASSOCIATION
Dispute Resolution Section

Cover design by Sara Wadford/ABA Design

Printed in the United States of America.

30 29 28 27 26   5 4 3 2 1

ISBN 978-1-63905-792-4

A catalog record for this book is available from the Library of Congress.

To my parents, Hong and Sukie Lee, who always encouraged me to write and follow my passion.

CONTENTS

ABOUT THE AUTHOR

Audrey J. Lee is a senior mediator at Boston Law Collaborative, LLC, and a lecturer on law at Harvard Law School, where she teaches courses on mediation and diversity & dispute resolution.

Audrey has mediated or coached hundreds of workplace conflicts over the last two decades. Since 2016, she has served as affiliate faculty at the Program on Negotiation at Harvard Law School, currently as a lead faculty for the Harvard Mediation Intensive. Previously, she has served as a mediator for the Massachusetts Commission Against Discrimination and as a panel mediator for the U.S. Equal Employment Opportunity Commission. In her mediations, Audrey draws on her experience as a consultant for the Cambridge, MA-based organization Essential Partners to bring a dialogue-centered approach to create spaces conducive to constructive learning.

In her consulting practice, Audrey works with clients to increase their effectiveness in difficult workplace conversations and negotiations. In recognition of her professional development work with lawyers, she was invited in 2018 to become a trusted advisor for the Professional Development Consortium, the national association for individuals responsible for the professional development of lawyers at law firms, law schools, government agencies, and corporations.

As a mediator and conflict management consultant, Audrey has worked with clients including lawyers at Am Law 100 firms, mediators at the Australian Fair Work Commission, and musicians at the League of American Orchestras. She has been featured in Harvard Business Review's "Insights" series on Leadership and Managing People and in the BBC Capital's Work Ethic column, and her writing on mediation and dispute resolution has appeared in the *Harvard Negotiation Law Review*, *Pepperdine Dispute Resolution Law Journal*, and *ABA Dispute Resolution Magazine*, among other publications. She is a graduate of Harvard College and Harvard Law School. She lives in Boston, where in her spare time she often finds herself mediating her children's sibling conflicts.

INTRODUCTION

You recently completed mediation training, so you're thrilled to be asked to mediate your first workplace case. But you have a million questions. Where do you turn?

Or maybe you've been mediating for some time but just wrapped up a case with one (or a few) unexpected twists. You'd love to debrief with a colleague to talk through how you handled things and what other approaches you might consider the next time. But you're drawing a blank on whom to contact.

Or you're an attorney who wants to give some pointers to a client about how best to handle a simmering employee conflict and avoid a discrimination complaint.

Or perhaps as HR or department head, you're not sure whether to deal with the latest internal conflict on your own or seek outside help. You've heard about mediation, but isn't that just for court cases?

If any of this sounds familiar, this book is for you.

We all encounter frustrating situations at work that we either avoid (often to our own detriment) or engage with in ways that might not be as productive as we'd like. In the last 20 years, I have mediated, coached, and trained hundreds of people in how to better approach workplace conflicts. Throughout this work, in my initial conversations with department heads, experienced counsel, and mediation trainees, people ask the same types of questions about workplace mediation. The facts vary, but the questions all focus on several topics about the process and substance, from start to finish. What can you expect to get out of an "early" workplace mediation (one that occurs before an internal complaint or lawsuit is filed)? What happens if someone won't participate? If the process goes awry? What happens if the feuding employees finally come to some agreement? Who's responsible for enforcing it? Because these questions are so common, using them to organize this book makes sense.

My goal for this book is that it will be a practical resource for several groups of people before, during, and after disagreements are addressed. Whether you're trying to resolve your own conflict or coach someone else with theirs, an HR leader searching for outside help for the first time, or a mediator aiming to turn your focus to workplace conflict, I hope that in this book you'll find both information and encouragement.

A note on terms. Conflict means different things to different people. Some may think of conflicts as intense, protracted disputes, perhaps on the battlefield or in court. For this book, I define a conflict as any conversation or relationship where the people involved experience friction or tension. This could be any workplace conversation that the participants find challenging for any reason. Perhaps it's a discussion they've put off for months. Or maybe it's one they've had many times, with much frustration and no good outcome. Maybe a supervisor and direct report have always had trouble talking, and this encounter is no exception. Or perhaps it's a conversation that focuses on one of those topics everyone dislikes talking about. Or it could be a dynamic where one or both coworkers are emotional—either solely as a result of the conflict or, as often happens, because a snowstorm of work and personal challenges is hitting one (or both) colleagues at the same time. All these qualify as conflict. (Many disagreements, especially in today's workplaces, involve teams and more than two parties. Those are well worth understanding and addressing, but to keep this book to a reasonable length, I am limiting my main focus to one-on-one workplace conflicts and mediations.)

I have tried to arrange the material so that it can be read from start to finish or consulted at specific points in the process, whether that's during mediation preparation or when some new question or challenge pops up. Or after it's over. As mediators know, thinking through what happened and what might have been done differently can bring big benefits down the road.

Part 1 of this book explores what workplace conflict is and how it differs from the many other kinds of conflict mediators and their clients encounter. It also includes suggestions for how to approach difficult workplace conversations on your own or how you might support a colleague or client to help them navigate their conflicts more skillfully. Then in Part 2 it moves to a discussion of the process of mediation, identifying points at which questions or specific challenges can surface. While much of the book is written for anyone interested in better understanding the workplace mediation process, the few sections on mediator practice tips will provide additional context for mediation participants as well. For increased readability, I have chosen to include footnotes sparingly, and for those interested in learning more, I have included all referenced resources in the Bibliography. Appendices provide additional detail, resources for mediators (continuing ed and reading), and sample templates.

A final note about the stories here: The examples included in the book derive from actual mediation cases, but to protect confidentiality I have changed some details and descriptions. In many instances, the examples reflect themes and challenges from multiple cases. And although I am a lawyer, I do not intend any portion of this book to be taken as legal advice.

PART 1

Understanding Workplace Conflict

1

What Is Workplace Conflict?

"What do you do?"

It's a common first question, whether we're greeting a new neighbor, chatting with someone in the bleachers at a youth soccer game, or socializing with strangers at a wedding. We define ourselves by our job titles. "I'm a teacher," your new acquaintance might say, or "I'm in IT." Even if we have a more holistic sense of self, others might not see us that way, at least not at first.

When we work, we often do so in the company of other people. And whenever people gather, disagreements are bound to come up. Conflict at work is actually on the rise. According to a 2022 Myers-Briggs Company report on workplace conflict, the time people spend on workplace conflict doubled between 2008 and 2022—and now, over a third report dealing with disputes often or even all the time.[1] Not surprisingly, the more time an employee spent dealing with conflict at work, the lower their job satisfaction and feeling of inclusion at work. So because work is a necessary part of life—except for those lucky enough to have a huge inheritance or win the lottery—workplace conflict is both inevitable and unpleasant.

1. The Myers-Briggs Company, *Conflict at Work* 16–17 (August 2022), https://www.themyersbriggs.com/-/media/Myers-Briggs/Files/Resources-Hub-Files/Research/TKI-Research-Report.pdf.

The disputes we have with coworkers, bosses, clients, and customers are similar to those we experience with family members or friends, but they're also different in significant ways. They can be particularly intense (and require specific skills to address), because for many of us, what we do—and how we are seen by our colleagues—strike at the core of our identity.

And, of course, a paycheck is how we support ourselves and our families. Whether we love or hate our work, it pays the bills. So any work conflict that might jeopardize our positions (and therefore our financial security) will probably weigh heavily on our minds. Add to that business pressures, supervisors' need to please their bosses or shareholders (or both), and the challenges inherent in teamwork, and you can have a real pressure cooker.

Given all this, the fact that workplace conflicts affect us in unique ways should come as no surprise. Because the stakes are high, we might first choose to ignore a small dispute, thinking we don't want to make it worse. But then the delay allows the conflict to fester. Or if we do engage, we might do so at the point where we feel pushed to a breaking point, stressed enough that what we say—and *how* we say it—is done hastily, without the benefit of thoughtful preparation and purpose. Either approach, delaying or acting out of frustration, can make the situation worse. No wonder workplace conflicts often feel fraught with danger and risk.

But there is hope. Choosing to engage—and to engage early—can be a huge positive step. Being self-aware and developing a few skills and techniques can keep difficult conversations from mushrooming into big messes. And for conflicts and difficult dynamics that early engagement and careful preparation don't or can't ease, getting help from an external impartial individual—namely, a mediator—can change things for the better.

Mediators sometimes work with opponents who glare across the conference table at each other, but not always. A mediator can consult with each person separately, to help him, her, or them prepare: "What are you really trying to get across?" the mediator might ask. Or "how could you say that in a way that won't be hard for your boss to hear?" A mediator can also just make things easier by facilitating conversation between colleagues, helping all those present understand what's been said, explore real interests and intentions, offer encouragement, and help everyone brainstorm about next steps.

So: Once an employee or client (or you yourself) is in a tricky workplace conflict, what should that person do? If someone on the sidelines wants to help, what's a good start? The next chapter provides information on how to prepare strategically and thoughtfully to engage in a constructive conversation to improve a challenging workplace dynamic.

2

How Can Someone Prepare for a Challenging Workplace Conversation?

In working with hundreds of people who are confronting strained working relationships and tense workplace conversations, I've seen several approaches that enable better outcomes. All of them start with preparation, perhaps best captured by one question: If challenging conversations are always going to be part of any workplace, how can an employee or boss be ready for them?

Imagine you have a colleague, direct report, or client who has been having trouble supervising an analyst. The two have worked together for months and the manager has offered constructive feedback, but to no avail: The analyst's work continues to be sloppy, missing important details and deadlines. The manager is fed up and starting to turn to other employees to get the work done.

This may sound like an everyday scenario, but imagine that other factors are complicating matters: Perhaps there is an age or gender difference, or maybe the two coworkers come from different racial or economic backgrounds. In the absence of clear communication, the analyst could think the sudden lack of work and feedback are connected to identity, and if the situation continues, the analyst might reach out to Human Resources and raise the possibility of filing a complaint about discrimination. The analyst might start talking to other colleagues. People might take sides, causing disruption and distraction. And things could get worse.

As a coach and mediator, I have seen this scenario and others like it many times. Because people look for help with a workplace conflict at different stages—of the conflict itself as well as their own readiness to do some work—it's critical for a coach or mediator to meet people where they are. We've all had the experience of turning to someone for help and having them really miss the mark—either they pile things on too much or they fail to realize you just needed some empathy before they start to problem-solve. So, even the most skillful coaching (or mediating) will land better if it's tailored to what the recipient can take in at that moment. And what a person can take in or even wants from a coach or mediator may evolve over time.

When I serve as a coach, individuals usually bring a challenging workplace conversation for us to explore together. In these situations, the conflict is typically at an earlier stage, before the time of an official complaint or disciplinary action. But other times, the disagreement is further along, with tension high enough that the two individuals can't even speak to each other, and I'm called in to help them through mediation. In both scenarios, I have found an approach that helps the employees involved get some insight into what's causing the challenging dynamic and consider ideas for approaching conversations more constructively.

(A brief acknowledgment here: Not everyone comes to coaching or mediation willingly or fearlessly. Many people who are told to get coaching or are ordered to participate in mediation, especially those who have gotten stuck in long-standing disputes, might start the process feeling angry, indignant, offended, or even embarrassed. Dealing with these emotions and meeting people where they are is a crucial part of establishing trust, and I'll discuss this further in Chapter 16, which addresses the idea of the process being voluntary, and Chapter 22, which covers strong emotions.) Once someone has agreed to participate, I generally set out five areas to explore in preparing for and managing a challenging workplace conflict. This list is like a menu: For any one conflict, one or two areas may be most salient. I encourage people to pick and choose.

1. **Interests.** What's most important to the people in the conversation?
2. **Partisan perceptions.** How might people see things a bit differently based on their past experiences?
3. **Relationship.** How can the working relationship be strengthened?
4. **Inquiry.** What would be helpful to learn?
5. **Advocacy.** How can one person best influence the other?

Looking through the lens of approaching a conflict directly on your own or as a coach supporting a colleague facing a conflict, here's more detail.

1. Identify interests

As students of negotiation know from the groundbreaking book *Getting to Yes*, people in a negotiation often start off by stating their positions. And those positions are often extreme. "He's an idiot," an employee might declare. "I never want to see him again." As mediators and others familiar with dispute resolution know very well, more conversation and careful questioning might end with the same employee explaining that he felt publicly humiliated by a recent interaction with his coworker. He respects this colleague, he says, but he can't forgive her behavior and wants some acknowledgment of wrongdoing. His real interest? What he really wants, he might eventually say, is some acknowledgment of harm—an apology. In public. And a promise that she won't insult him again in front of others. Although an everyday workplace or business conversation may not seem like a negotiation, applying the same "negotiation" analysis to workplace conversations, with attention to positions and interests, is often a useful exercise.

For someone in conflict or in counseling a colleague in conflict, you might consider the following:

- What is most important to you?
- In this working relationship or this particular conversation, what are your goals or priorities?

The next step is to apply these same questions to the *other* person in the dispute or difficult conversation. We've all heard about the value of walking a mile in someone's shoes. That's an old adage, but it's applicable here. Considering what you know—or imagine—to be your counterpart's interests can actually be in your own interest, if only because it can help you get what you need.

2. Explore perceptions

One way to think about exploring perceptions is to use a tool called the Ladder of Inference. The Ladder of Inference, created by organizational behaviorists Chris Argyris of Harvard Business School and Donald Schon of MIT, is a simplified way to understand how our brains process new information and help map how people make decisions.

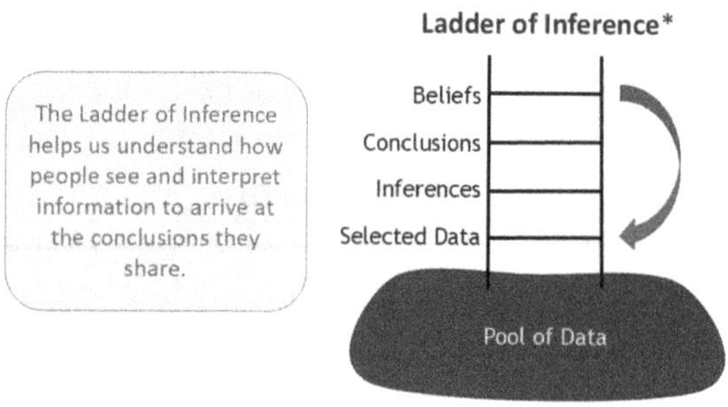

*Developed by Chris Argyris of Harvard Business School and Donald Schon of MIT.

At the bottom of the Ladder, we see a pool of data representing millions of bits of information that surround us at any given moment. From there, our brains select a very tiny fraction of that available information for us to notice. What we notice is influenced by our life experiences—our professional experiences and personal history affect what might be important or relevant or interesting to us. From there, we tell ourselves a story or attach meaning to the data points that we have noticed. This part of the process is also highly influenced by our past experiences and informs our conclusions. A conclusion could take different forms—an opinion about a colleague, a recommendation to a client, or a business decision. What is challenging here is that we know from research in psychology that once we have formed a conclusion or an opinion over time, we tend to be subject to confirmation bias; in other words, we give value to new information that confirms what we already believe and less credence to new information that counters our pre-existing views.

We can apply this thinking to challenging workplace conversations to consider how we are seeing a given situation, the other person involved, and the dynamics at play. This approach invites us to think about how, if we stood in the shoes of our counterpart, he or she might be seeing us in the conversation or in the time before the present day. Some questions we might ask ourselves include:

- What story am I telling myself about this situation?
- How might I explain what's going on to a trusted friend or confidant?
- What past experiences might be helpful to consider in thinking about how I'm seeing this conversation or this coworker?
- What information might I be missing or overlooking (that might suggest a different interpretation)?

And just as with interests, seeing the situation through the other person's eyes, imagining what that person's perceptions might be about you and the situation, can be very helpful.

3. Strengthen the relationship

The next area for possible consideration is thinking about how to strengthen the working relationship. One way to approach this is to conduct a "relationship audit" and reflect on a few key questions. Starting with the current relationship:

Current Working Relationship

- What is the working relationship like now?
- What adjectives would you use to describe it?
- Why might the relationship be the way it is presently?

(This last question involves a bit of reflection—and diagnosis—but it's worth the work.)

Thinking about what the relationship might look like in the future can help someone get unstuck from the bothersome present. To get there, try this:

Future Preferred Working Relationship

- If your working relationship could be improved in some way, six months (or maybe five years) from now, what might that look like? What might be a positive change for working together or communicating?
- With that improved relationship as a goal, what general strategies or ideas could nudge the working relationship in that direction?
- Given these general ideas for improvement, what action items could advance your strategies? How about starting with just one move? What one action could you take tomorrow (or next week or next month) that could help move things in the right direction?

4. Inquire to understand and learn

After considering what's most important to both people in the conversation, how perceptions may vary, and how those involved might improve their working relationship, you can move onto what might be said or done in this difficult conversation. For this, try focusing on inquiry, imagining which questions might be helpful to learn more about the other person's interests and how they're seeing things. After that, the focus will be on advocating for your own interests.

First, inquiry. The term means asking genuinely curious questions. But what is a genuinely curious question? One way to think of it is a question whose answer the questioner doesn't know. Perhaps such questions can spring out of the earlier discussion about identifying interests, perceptions, and hopes for the future relationship. At times, another type of inquiry might be aimed at better understanding or learning the other person's preferences about communication. How does the person like to be contacted? How often? What's the person's preferred way to conduct important conversations? Genuine inquiry shows interest in learning about the other person, which often leads the person on the receiving end to want to learn more, too.

5. Advocate to influence

Advocacy here means thinking about how best to advance your own interests based on what you know (or can imagine) about your counterpart's interests and perceptions. In other words, how to say what you want to say in the way that the recipient will best hear and understand it. More specifically, how can you best communicate what's important to you to the other person? How will you open the conversation? Is it possible that one of your interests might even be aligned with those of the other person and you can frame your message to highlight that shared interest? Brainstorming about interests and advocacy can make some people see common interests—even if only that the status quo is untenable—where once they saw only a battleground.

***

With all this in mind, think back to the workplace situation that opened this chapter, that of the analyst and boss.

In more detail: Morgan, age 36, has been a manager for five years and an employee for nine years. She supervises Alex, who is 52 and has worked for the company for only four years. After a re-org about nine months ago, they started working together. Over the last several months, Morgan has been frustrated by what she sees as Alex's continued sloppy work and apparent refusal to listen to her feedback. She's so frustrated, in fact, that she's stopped trying to work with Alex and has been taking the assignments to others for efficiency reasons. Alex, on the other hand, is confused about why Morgan has suddenly stopped talking to him and giving him regular assignments. His annual performance reviews with his past manager have been positive, and he thought things were going well enough with Morgan (who is much more hands-on than his last manager). Because he feels he has never heard exactly why his work is not satisfactory, Alex is increasingly concerned that his reputation—and possibly, his job—are in jeopardy for reasons that have nothing to do with performance. In a recent visit to HR, he wondered whether Morgan is avoiding him and not giving him work because of his age.

Interests

Imagine that you are coaching the manager, Morgan, on how to improve things with Alex. You could start with the following questions:

- *Morgan's Interests.* In your conflict with Alex and more generally, what's important to you? What are your interests?
- *Alex's Interests.* What do you think might be important to Alex? In this conversation about feedback and more generally?

You could capture Morgan's interests as follows, along with her educated guesses as to Alex's interests:

Morgan's Interests (according to Morgan)	**Alex's Interests** (according to Morgan)
Get work done	Reputation (competence)
Peace of mind	Job security
Minimize time redoing work	Work efficiently
Reputation (good manager)	Build relationships

Imagining that Morgan has made accurate guesses about Alex's interests, we can see a few shared interests, namely maintaining a positive reputation and getting work done efficiently.

Perceptions

In this second area of prep, you could invite Morgan to think about past background-related experiences that might shed light on or be relevant to the current conversation. You can capture Morgan's perceptions as follows, along with her educated guesses as to Alex's perceptions:

Morgan's Perceptions (according to Morgan)	**Alex's Perceptions** (according to Morgan)
What have you learned from past feedback conversations that might be helpful to keep in mind? – People seem to respond better to receiving feedback when there are both positive and constructive pieces of feedback. – People were helpful in showing me the way when I was coming up.	*If you put yourself in Alex's shoes, how do you think he sees you?* – Morgan does not provide guidance or samples of what she wants, is not available for questions, and then is usually upset with my final product. – We don't really know each other very well on a personal level, either.
What have you experienced as a recipient of feedback that you'd like to keep in mind (to do or avoid)? – Specific examples are most helpful. – It is really terrible sometimes to receive unexpected negative feedback, but it's helpful to know where I stand and how I can try to do better. (When people do give tough feedback, it shows they care enough to take the time to do so, maybe showing an interest in helping me improve.)	*What might Alex tell a trusted friend about what he believes is really going on here?* – All of my past performance evaluations (with my past manager) have been positive. – Morgan's management style is different from my last manager's. – Things took a sudden turn awhile back, and now I am not getting any more work with Morgan. I am not sure why—is it because of my age?
What have you learned about working with Alex so far that might be helpful to keep in mind? What do you think is the best way to communicate with Alex? – Alex seems to appreciate getting a heads-up about a meeting so he can prepare in advance. He also prefers in-person communications.	

From this brainstorming, Morgan should be able to see that she and Alex have had different experiences in the workplace and that these divergent experiences might be a factor in their current conflict.

Relationship

Especially when two people expect or need to have a continuing relationship, engaging in some analysis of that relationship is helpful. For this area of prep, the idea is to think about the current state of the relationship and how to get to a preferred state of the relationship:

- What is the working relationship like now?
- How would you like to see it in the future (if there is a gap)?
- What steps can you take to move it in that direction?

We can pose these questions to Morgan and capture her responses using the following Circle Chart, a framework introduced in *Getting to Yes* for preparing and conducting negotiations or difficult conversations. The chart organizes four types of thinking as steps to be taken in sequence to address a problem. Its name comes from the fact that the first step begins in the bottom left quadrant, and the analysis moves in a circular fashion to end in the bottom right-hand quadrant. Here is how Morgan might use the Circle Chart to think about improving her working relationship with Alex:

II. Current Relationship—Diagnosis (Why?)	**III. Strategies to Improve**
– We don't have any personal relationship or interactions. – I have been annoyed and frustrated with Alex, so I have been avoiding him.	– Share my interest in developing him as a valued member of the team if he wants that (so I don't have to retrain someone, which is huge). – Get to know each other a bit more.
I. Current Relationship Status	**IV. Action Steps to Implement**
– Strained – Not active/engaged	– Reach out to find a time to chat and begin a conversation on these topics.

For an important ongoing working relationship, taking stock of its current state and brainstorming ways to cultivate and improve it are crucial steps in preparing for a difficult, important conversation.

Inquiry and advocacy

After brainstorming about interests, perceptions, and ways to improve the relationship, Morgan can turn to thinking about how to incorporate these ideas into the actual conversation. Remember: For inquiry, the focus is on questions that can help the questioner learn more about the other person's interests and perceptions. Advocacy involves thinking about the best way to get messages across to the other person, based on what the speaker knows or imagines might be the other person's interests and perceptions.

Here are questions (and Morgan's answers) that could help Morgan begin brainstorming how best to approach the conversation:

Inquiry	Advocacy
What genuinely curious questions can you ask Alex to learn more about his interests and perceptions? – How would you prefer to receive feedback? – What can we try differently in terms of working together? – Would it be helpful to walk through a project assignment together and/or show you what I am hoping to receive so I can then turn it around in a timely way to our partners? – Would it be helpful to plan to meet partway through a project to see how things are going?	*Knowing what you know about Alex, his probable interests and perceptions, as well as your own, what is the best way to communicate the messages you would like to share?* – I was really lucky to have people giving me helpful tips about how to succeed here and do things the "right way." – I would like for us both to be able to work as efficiently as possible. – If you need help or have a question, I really want to hear from you. It's actually better for both of us if we can talk about something earlier instead of at the last minute. (And if I was not as available before, I am sorry about that.)

If Morgan takes this entire prep session to heart, she should be able to engage in a productive conversation with Alex, perhaps turning the corner on a rough patch in their working relationship.

3

If the Workplace Dynamic Is a Particularly Difficult One, What Other Strategies Can Help?

What about workplace conflicts in which at least one person involved has little (or no) interest in talking about what's been going on, let alone fixing it? The prep strategies outlined so far can help improve any conversation, but challenging dynamics can complicate matters. These might include:

- The other person's responses are completely unhelpful.
- The other person is too emotional.
- The other person is your boss.

Let's take each of these scenarios in turn.

Difficult scenario #1: The other person's responses are completely unhelpful

In these situations, staying constructive can be an enormous challenge. One strategy to consider is reframing, which is the skill of transforming unproductive comments into useful, relevant pieces of information to help move the conversation forward. There are three approaches to reframing that might be helpful here:

1. Reframe from positions to interests.
2. Reframe from past to future.
3. Reframe from negative to positive.

Take, for example, the kind of mini verbal attack we've all heard in one form or another.

"You're such a micro-manager!" a direct report, boiling over with frustration, might spit out. Many managers would need a long moment to recover, and some would match insult for insult or walk away. But a manager who has been coached well—and encouraged to stay calm and curious instead of reacting—might be able to take a deep breath and reframe in several ways.

"Sounds like you want more autonomy in your work," that skilled manager might say quietly, reframing from position to interest. Or reframing from past to future: "So, going forward, you'd like to talk about a change in roles and responsibilities." Or reframe number three, from negative to positive: "OK. How about we sit down together and talk about redefining our roles and decision-making, so we can both be clear about who'll do what?" (This one has the added bonus of reframing to make the statement more collaborative and inclusive.)

This kind of reframing is a skill, but like most skills, it gets easier with practice.

Difficult scenario #2: The other person is too emotional

In many workplace settings, employees are told to "leave the emotions out of it" or "not get emotional" when facing a difficult conversation. However, as Douglas Stone, Bruce Patton, and Sheila Heen note in their book *Difficult Conversations*, we ignore emotions at our peril. Emotions have a way of finding their way into the conversation—in our tone, facial expressions, or reactions to an offhand comment—despite our best efforts to keep them out. Instead of fearing or trying to shut out the emotions, we can try to use emotional "feedback" as important information in our conversations and leverage positive emotions.

In *Beyond Reason: Using Emotions as You Negotiate*, Roger Fisher and Daniel Shapiro argue that keeping detailed track of emotions in a negotiation—yours and theirs—is a Herculean task. Acknowledging that we can't possibly keep all of them in our minds as we interact or negotiate with others, they distill these emotions into five Core Concerns or emotional interests:

- **Autonomy.** Do I have a sphere of influence that's my own for decision-making purposes?
- **Appreciation.** Am I recognized and acknowledged for my contributions and efforts?
- **Affiliation.** Am I in or out? Do I feel a sense of connection and belonging with others in the group?
- **Status.** Is my expertise or experience acknowledged and respected?
- **Role.** Do I have a role that's meaningful? Valued?

Considering the Core Concerns can be useful in navigating a conflict directly on your own or as a mediator assisting others in resolving their conflict. As described in *Beyond Reason*, the Core Concerns can be used as a lens to help diagnose what might be causing the tension, as well as a lever to shed light on what might be helpful for parties in conflict.

Strong emotions can show up in different ways. While most of us may think of shouting or tears when we hear about strong emotions, the quieter manifestation can be just as challenging.

MULTIPLE DEGREES

When Isaac, a mid-level manager in a management consulting firm, walked into the coaching room, the coach hired to help him immediately sensed a range of emotions from his proud demeanor and defiant glare: reluctance, frustration, and annoyance. After she invited him to talk about a workplace conflict for them to work on together, he stared intently at the coach, and after a brief pause, said he had none. He did not have any relationships or conversations at work that he felt were challenging for him. Here is the exchange that followed:

Coach: "Well, this time was designed to be used in whatever way you would find most helpful. How would you like to use the time?" [*role, autonomy*]

(continued)

(continued)

Isaac: (After a pause) "Like I said, I don't have any problems myself, but it is so frustrating that despite the fact that I've got multiple degrees from prestigious universities and have worked at jobs like this before, my colleagues don't value my expertise or thoughts on our projects."

Coach: "It sounds like you're trying to make a meaningful contribution to your work drawing on your past experiences." [*appreciation*]

Isaac: "Yes! This place is so hierarchical—the people here don't care if you have a good idea. They just want to follow the lead on the team."

Coach: "That sounds incredibly frustrating, especially when you feel like you have something to offer and you're trying to make a contribution based on your past experiences." [*appreciation, status*]

Isaac: "That's right! Actually, this reminds me of something that happened last week. . . ."

While this example involves the initial interaction between a coach and one colleague experiencing conflict in the workplace, the same analysis could apply to challenging interactions people experience directly: in a nutshell, what Core Concerns might be at play in this conflict for the other person?

Difficult scenario #3: The other person is your boss

Challenging workplace conversations are hard enough with peers, but when the two people involved are of different status, risks and emotions can skyrocket. In these situations, using the Core Concerns can also be a helpful strategy, particularly appreciation, status, and role.

If we are in conflict with someone, chances are we have not appreciated them, we are not honoring their expertise or status, and/or we are not giving them a positive or meaningful role. As the saying goes, "We are all the heroes in our own stories." When more than one Core Concern is unmet, tension rises.

MANAGING UP

Alejandro wants to give unsolicited feedback to his manager, Christina, about strategy on their current project, which involves a heavy amount of data analysis. This is the kind of work Alejandro did at his last firm, and he knows that there are more efficient ways to approach the analysis. But because he's acutely aware of the power imbalance, he hasn't yet raised the issue. From some past interactions with Christina, Alejandro has gathered that Christina likes to follow the chain of command, including deference to the more senior person. Alejandro is fine with that and feels like he has something to contribute here—if only he can figure out how to do it delicately. One approach might be for him to honor Christina's status as a manager and recast her in a different role. Keeping this in mind, here's how Alejandro could approach a conversation with Christina.

Alejandro: "I know we've been having some challenges with the project lately. Can we talk about it for a few minutes?"

Christina looks up from her laptop and nods.

Alejandro: "Well, based on your experience with this client and the director [*status*], I wonder how you think they would react to a slightly different approach."

Christina: "You know, there's a good reason we're doing it this way. . . ."

Alejandro: "I know I might not have the full picture, and I was hoping you could fill me in [*status*] on any developments. Could we take a few minutes for you to update me and for me to share what I've been noticing on the ground? I just want to make sure I'm flagging the right things—and that I have in mind the kinds of issues and ideas I should elevate to you for your review." [*role*]

Christina: "Sounds like it might be worth a few minutes. . . ."

In this example, the direct report is acknowledging the experience or status of the manager—both within the organization and with the particular client—and inviting the manager into a different role. If the direct report was seeing the manager as a barrier to change before, he is now recasting the manager as a collaborator or partner. It's a simple "move," but it's a shift (both mental and verbal) that could make the difference in nudging the relationship into a more productive space.

4

When Is It Time to Involve a Third Party?

In many workplace conflicts, one or both of the individuals involved may be well equipped to improve communication and the working relationship on their own or with the support of a colleague serving as an informal coach. However, there are some situations where direct engagement is not sufficient. Here are some indicators that involving an outside resource such as a mediator might be helpful:

- You have tried to facilitate or mediate the conflict with both employees, but nothing has changed.
- You have tried to coach your colleagues separately, with no improvement.
- A disciplinary action is on the horizon or has just occurred for one or both employees.
- One of the people in conflict has asked about the process of filing an internal complaint.
- You have learned that the conflict is affecting others.
- You have become close to one of the people involved, which could make one or both believe you'll be biased.
- Your personal feelings or views are limiting your ability to help.

- The employer's internal conflict management resource—a mediator, coach, or ombuds (an independent, impartial, confidential and informal resource)—has worked with the parties, but the stalemate continues.

If one of these scenarios has unfolded in your organization, the time might be right to learn more about using an external mediator. If this idea is a new one, you might want to talk with a trusted and knowledgeable partner such as Human Resources or employment counsel about whether mediation is the right way to go.

In Part 2, I identify 25 questions people often ask about the mediation process from start to finish.

PART 2

Mediating Workplace Conflicts

Here is where things stand: A conflict has persisted, and efforts to resolve the disagreement—or maybe even just lower the temperature in the office—haven't worked. A supervisor, a department head, or an HR leader has decided to ask an outside mediator for help. Questions are sure to come up about the process and purpose of mediation as well as topics related to the specific conflict or parties' needs. This book is organized chronologically according to the life span of a mediation. For ease of reference, this part has been further divided into three sections: Getting Started, In the Mediation: Managing Parties and the Process, and Wrapping Up.

Other resources cover the general subject of mediation, and they're always helpful, but my focus here is examining how workplace mediations differ from more traditional ones that take place when litigation is underway or possible. Taken together, the chapters can serve as an overview, but each chapter is also designed to be a stand-alone guide to a particular question or subject.

Let's take each topic in turn.

Getting Started

5

What Is the Purpose or Goal of a Workplace Mediation?

When I tell people I mediate workplace cases, they often respond with confused looks. "I thought mediation was for cases in court," some say, or "That doesn't make sense. What kind of outcome do you have if there's no complaint?" These cases generally don't follow the more traditional mediation route that ends in signed settlement agreements with money changing hands, the outcome most lawyers and clients imagine for cases in litigation. Instead, the purpose of a workplace mediation may be to help the people (meaning the coworkers) involved:

- Move forward productively.
- Address tension stemming from past difficult interactions or conversations.
- Exchange perspectives and hopes for the future working relationship.
- Reconcile conflicting personalities or communication preferences.
- Understand the impact of past difficult interactions on each person.

Accordingly, possible outcomes of a workplace mediation may include agreements on:

- How to communicate in the future (e.g., Is email better than phone calls or in-person meetings? How often should communication happen?).
- How to allocate or confirm roles and responsibilities.
- How to give and get feedback.
- How to initiate future difficult conversations.
- How to determine whether the processes and approaches are working and whether they need to be adapted.
- How and when to meet again—and how to determine agenda items for meetings.
- How these discussions and progress in general will be communicated to others in the workplace (e.g., up, down, and sideways in the org chart).

Sometimes, however, the "outcome" is the process itself—a facilitated space where two or more people can exchange perspectives, experiences, and hopes for the future. An outcome may also involve a better understanding or appreciation of the other person and where they're coming from.

In short, a primary purpose of workplace mediation is to improve two colleagues' relationship, communication, and productivity. Sometimes this may involve a goal to better understand each other or mutual understanding of each other's perspectives. The outcome will depend on what the two people involved believe will help support a change in their working dynamic.

What is a "successful" mediation?

How will the people involved, their bosses or HR officials, and the mediator know whether the process has been effective? Many lawyers, mediators, and would-be participants might define success as an agreement. Agreements do happen, but other metrics warrant consideration, particularly when a workplace conflict is in the early stages. In these cases, if no complaint or court case is likely, there may be no need for a formal settlement agreement.

Here are some other indicators of a successful workplace mediation:

- Parties can exchange and process information to help them make more informed decisions about next steps.
- Each person comes away with an increased understanding of the other's perspective on past challenging interactions or events.
- Parties brainstorm and agree on ideas for how to move forward.
- One or both parties feel heard in the process (by the other person, the mediator, or both).
- Parties are able to communicate productively going forward.

Other indicators of success might also include the following post-mediation possibilities:

- Any agreements coming out of the mediation are honored.
- In post-mediation feedback forms, parties express satisfaction with the experience.
- Parties recommend mediation to others in the organization.

But sometimes success can come in surprising forms. Consider the following:

TOO EXHAUSTED TO PARTICIPATE

Like many mediators, Olivia offers brief informational conversations to parties who are considering working with her in mediation, so she begins this case by speaking with Braden and Kenji, two employees who have been feuding for many months. Because Braden is on leave and Olivia has been told that he might not be able to participate in mediation, she begins with him.

But scheduling time for this first talk with Braden is difficult, and when Olivia does finally reach him at home, he tells her he's taking time off to recover from an intense, emotionally draining, yearlong dispute with Kenji. Months of intense bullying by Kenji, he says, have left him exhausted and isolated, and now he isn't sure that he can even be in the same room (actual or virtual) as Kenji, let alone summon the mental strength to engage in what he knows would be an intensely difficult conversation, even with the help of a mediator.

(continued)

(continued)

After talking for about half an hour, Braden and the mediator agree that the process simply shouldn't happen. Maybe sometime down the road the two coworkers can meet and talk about their experience, but not now. And so the mediation ends after this pre-mediation discussion.

At the close of their conversation, Braden tells Olivia that he's had numerous conversations with the organization's director and human resources manager, but this is the first time he has felt truly heard, and he is very grateful.

For Olivia, this is a successful mediation she'll remember.

6

Mediation, Facilitation, Climate Assessment, Dialogue—Which One Is the Right Process?

During an intake conversation, employer contacts, supervisors, or HR officials commonly ask about process. Given this particular conflict, is mediation the right fit? Would another process such as facilitation or a climate assessment be more appropriate?

For some, the word *mediation* immediately brings to mind a legal battle. (Chapters 5 and 8 about the goals and processes of workplace mediation might dispel that image.) For others, seeking mediation or referring someone to it might be viewed as a vote of no confidence, a sign that someone—maybe one of the people involved or a boss—is in over his or her head, unable to resolve the problem. With these associations, it's no surprise that some gravitate toward facilitation.

Facilitation is the process by which a third party assists a group in achieving a shared goal. Board retreats, for example, often bring in a facilitator to help leaders discuss how they'd like to execute their vision or implement strategic plans. Mediation, by contrast, is often defined as assisted negotiation, a process by which the mediator helps people reach a resolution that they find acceptable, one that meets their underlying needs and interests.

Both processes can be helpful, but many people prefer mediation for the confidentiality it affords. As mediator and Harvard Law School Lecturer on Law David Hoffman explains in his book *Mediation: A Practice Guide for Mediators, Lawyers, and Other Professionals*, mediation confidentiality is provided by statute (e.g., in Massachusetts, by G.L. ch. 233, § 23C, or in some states by the Uniform Mediation Act), procedural rules created by courts, ethical duties of the mediator, and Agreements to Mediate. Agreements to Mediate, usually signed by all participants at the start of mediation, typically outline the scope of confidentiality and exceptions to confidentiality. The confidentiality terms of such agreements usually extend to both oral and written communications by the mediator and the parties.

An Agreement to Mediate can also include exceptions to confidentiality—for example, the parties may want to be able to disclose what happens in mediation to their lawyers, therapists, spouses, financial advisors, or business partners. Mediators may also include exceptions to confidentiality permitting, but not requiring, disclosure by the mediator or parties of information relating to the risk of serious harm to an individual or child or elder abuse or neglect, for example.

If the conflict is one where confidentiality would be valuable—if litigation is looming or privacy is paramount—mediation may be the better option. And if someone is wary of mediation because they connect it with legal processes, the mediator can explain the difference between mediations for workplace cases and for those that are in the process of being litigated.

What is a climate assessment? How does it compare to mediation?

Some disputes are signs of more systemic issues. Several years ago, I was asked to help with a conflict in a company I had worked with before. This dispute, the department head said, sounded similar to the earlier case: Two colleagues had been fighting so long that their dysfunctional relationship was affecting everyone around them—and even people in other departments they dealt with. As the department head described the problem, he mentioned broader issues: Managers wanted more input in decisions made by senior directors, a spokesperson who could advocate for them, and the ability to voice opinions that differed from their superiors. In short, trust and morale were near rock bottom. Given all of this, I suggested that a different, larger-scope intervention was needed. While a mediation might help the two people, until the systemic problems were addressed, disagreements would surely persist. A climate assessment, we concluded, was the right fit.

According to mediator and climate assessment expert Loraine Della Porta, a climate assessment takes "the pulse of an organization and provides leadership with feedback by identifying areas of strength and areas in need of improvement."[1] In this process, an outside facilitator (or team of facilitators) first attempts to understand the root causes of the challenges in a workplace, team, or group through confidential one-on-one conversations. In the same spirit of confidentiality as in mediation, all participants understand that the facilitator will protect the confidentiality of what is said in the individual discussions and share only aggregate themes with the organization's leaders and the larger team. Based on what she learns from the conversations, the facilitator then suggests other interventions that might improve the existing dynamics.

Phase 1 of a climate assessment may include the following steps:

- Identify all stakeholders who should be included in confidential interviews with the facilitator.
- Share a welcome message with this group of stakeholders, outlining the process steps of the assessment and reiterating the confidentiality of the process.
- Prepare and share a climate assessment participation agreement with each person involved, to confirm expectations and commitments to the process.
- Conduct confidential one-on-one interviews using an interview protocol or set of questions for consistency across interview conversations.

1. Loraine Della Porta, "Do You Need an Organizational Climate Assessment?" The Mediation Group (May 23, 2023), https://www.themediationgroup.org/blog-posts/do-you-need-an-organizational-climate-assessment.

After these conversations, the facilitator might suggest various interventions, including:

- Two-party mediation.
- Large-group facilitation.
- Facilitation of team or department meeting by an outside professional.
- Facilitated community discussions.
- Skills-based trainings on topics such as managing conflict, giving effective feedback, communicating across differences, and teaching mediation skills to managers.
- Individual coaching.

Through a variety of complementary interventions, the goal in Phase 2 of a climate assessment is to provide support for the participants to learn and practice new skills, experience different ways of communicating and interacting more productively, and support the group's behavioral changes or evolving norms toward the desired changes as identified in the Phase 1 interviews.

When is a climate assessment the right choice? It's helpful when multiple members of a work team are involved (such as several managers in one department), or when several individuals are affected by one event (such as a loud ongoing disagreement between two coworkers), or an underlying dynamic (such as lack or trust) has negatively impacted a group. Because it offers the scaffolding of various interventions to support changed behavior, a climate assessment may be a better way to repair damage to a group, team, or department, as compared to mediation.

How is workplace mediation different from dialogue?

If a goal of many workplace mediations is to promote understanding between the parties, the process of dialogue can help. John Sarrouf, co-executive director of Essential Partners (formerly known as the Public Conversations Project), a leader in the field, describes the goal of dialogue as the pursuit of "mutual understanding and improved communication that enhances curiosity, respect, and trust."[2]

With this in mind, Essential Partners has developed a framework to interrupt dysfunctional dynamics and build relationships across differences. Reflective Structured Dialogue centers around providing people with different experiences and varying formal or structural power an opportunity to share experiences and deepen understanding of each other. In a recent Essential Partners Dialogic classroom training for higher ed educators, the functions of dialogue were described as follows:

- Promote mutual understanding.
- Encourage people to connect with experience.
- Encourage self-reflection.
- Recommend multiple perspectives.
- Raise curiosity.
- Improve communication skills.

Not listed? Problem-solving and decision-making. This is a key difference between the two processes of dialogue and mediation. While a workplace mediation and dialogue may both include dialogic practices (more on this in Chapter 23), the mediation may also include agreements about how the parties want to move forward together, as described in Chapter 5.

2. John Sarrouf, *In Pursuit of the Dialogic Classroom: Designing Spaces for Conviction*, *in* Bias, Belief, and Conviction in an Age of Fake Facts 184 (2022).

7

When Is the Best Time to Try Mediation?

Imagine the following:

- Two colleagues who work in the same open-plan area have not been speaking for some time, and things have gotten so unpleasant that when they do need to communicate, they have to use email or call in a third person to keep things civil.
- One week after a heated argument, a manager and her direct report have exchanged only a few tense words—and now the direct report has asked for a meeting with HR.
- HR has begun to investigate a complaint of discrimination involving two coworkers.

On paper, any of these scenarios looks right for mediation, but, in practice, certain situations—or rather, specific times in the life cycle of a conflict—may be better suited to mediation.

To understand when mediation may be most helpful, consider how a mediator is brought into a matter in the first place. Unlike more traditional mediations, in workplace mediations, the employer (or someone acting on the employer's behalf) is typically the one who first contacts the mediator and pays for the mediator's services. Because everyone knows this, it's important for the mediator to be clear with all involved—the parties, the mediator's contact, and others—that even though the employer is footing the bill, the mediator will be impartial and hold what is said in the mediation in confidence, perhaps sharing only scheduling updates with the employer contact. This might not be easy to do, but the goal is simple: to protect the integrity of the mediation process. To do this, the mediator must establish clear boundaries about sharing information.

Timing matters, too. Mediating before the start of a formal disciplinary process, such as an investigation, is helpful because at that point parties may feel they can be more candid in conversations with the mediator (pre-mediation and during the mediation itself) without worrying that their words will work their way into the disciplinary process. This should not be a concern because mediation is a confidential process, but uncertainty or fear about the level of confidentiality may still constrain parties.

Another advantage of mediating early is that the mediator and parties may be more likely to have the same information. If a disciplinary process is already underway, for example, the employer contact may decide to share information about that process with the mediator, who then will probably know more about it than the people involved. This might be helpful for the mediator's general understanding, but it can be awkward if one of the parties asks questions about the process that the mediator can't answer. (One way to avoid this is for the mediator to set another boundary and ask the employer contact to relay only news about the disciplinary process that the parties get, too.)

Are there some instances—because of timing or other factors—when a case should not be mediated?

If you ask a newly trained mediator if they'd like to take on a new case, chances are they'll say yes quickly and enthusiastically. As many newly minted mediators can attest, getting cases, especially early on, is difficult, and even volunteering to mediate—whether in a court program or otherwise—is not a guarantee of cases. Many new mediators, drawn to the field by a desire to help others resolve differences amicably, may also think that all (or almost all) cases should be mediated. (Time and experience can change that view.)

Even if all parties are interested in trying mediation, a few considerations may cause a mediator to decide to decline a mediation or suggest another process. These include workplace issues that affect an entire division or group, not just two individuals; one party's insistence that a third party, perhaps her manager, should be present in mediation, but that person doesn't want to participate; or serious concerns about safety.

If a case involves a history of physical violence or threats of violence, would that case be appropriate for mediation? What if the mediator learns of this in pre-mediation calls, once the mediation has begun? Even if the party who has felt threatened wants to mediate, a mediator may think that there is a real risk to physical safety and choose not to take the case—or, if the case has started, to withdraw. (Even if the mediator does decline or withdraw, he or she should check in with the party who felt threatened, to confirm that they have the support or resources they need if they feel at risk in the future.)

8

What Does the Mediation Process Look Like?

When an employer contact or parties first meet with the mediator, many start by asking about process and timing. When can parties expect the process to begin? What will it look like? How long does it take? The answers, in short, describe the two steps in most workplace mediations: the pre-mediation conversations and the actual mediation sessions.

Pre-mediation conversations

Most mediators conduct one-on-one confidential pre-mediation conversations with each party. Before the COVID pandemic, these conversations were conducted almost exclusively by phone, which usually was more convenient than in-person meetings; post-pandemic, many parties and mediators opt to connect for the first time via Zoom. The purpose of these discussions is multifold: They serve as a chance for the mediator to introduce herself, share information about the mediation process, answer questions, and learn directly from each person about background events and their goals for the mediation. Typically, these conversations last between 30 and 60 minutes, although some last longer or move more quickly. (See Chapter 12 for more information on pre-mediation calls.)

First mediation session

Before COVID changed the way so many people work, after conducting pre-mediation conversations, many workplace mediators scheduled a half day mediation session that typically lasted three or four hours. Today a more common approach is to schedule a shorter session, usually one that lasts 90 minutes to two hours, with the possibility or even expectation of having one or more follow-up sessions. Shorter sessions are advisable for several reasons, most notably because they're easier to schedule and tend to be more manageable for people who are feeling stressed. Two primary objectives for the initial session are to surface each party's goals for the mediation and begin or reset constructive dialogue.

It's also important for the mediator to provide clarity about the process as she begins the first session. While it might be tempting to give a process overview short shrift, studies of workplace mediation have shown that people are more satisfied with mediation when they perceive that procedures have been fair. Based on their analysis of workplace mediations, University of Leuven researcher Katalien Bollen and professor Martin Euwema identified the following factors as contributing to parties believing the process is procedurally just: The parties have an opportunity to participate in the process; they have some control or input over the process; they believe the process is impartial; and they believe that they've been treated with respect. Their finding on the importance of procedural justice to workplace mediation parties aligns with broader research on this topic. In their book, *Psychology for Lawyers*, University of Illinois professor of law and psychology Jennifer Robbennolt and University of Nevada Las Vegas law professor Jean Sternlight note the significant impact of the parties' perception of fairness in a variety of contexts including mediation generally as well as litigation and arbitration; if the parties believe the process is fair, they are more likely to believe the outcome is fair (even if it falls short of their ideal).

A first mediation session may include both joint sessions and private sessions or caucuses. Most workplace mediations, like many other mediations, start with a joint session, with the mediator and parties together, so the mediator can give opening remarks and begin a conversation. Later, the mediator may find it useful to have a round (or multiple rounds) of private sessions in which she meets individually with each person as a way to move the conversation forward. (More on caucuses later.)

This is the general pattern of many mediators who deal with workplace conflict, but it's important to note that each mediator has her own style, and any one mediator may approach the process differently. In their study of 1,065 mediators in civil and family cases, Rochelle Wissler, a researcher at Arizona State University's Sandra Day O'Connor College of Law, and Art Hinshaw, a professor and dean there, found that most mediators use the same structure—initial joint session or initial caucuses—in most or all of their cases, regardless of certain factors that might suggest one route over the other. Surprisingly, factors such as a past or continuing relationship, nonmonetary or broader issues, unusually emotional parties, or alleged harassment, for example, did not influence the mediators' process decision. So it may be important to learn about a mediator's style (as discussed in Chapter 9) if there are important process preferences for a given case.

Second mediation session

After the initial mediation session, scheduling a follow-up session can be helpful. Before any second session, however, the mediator may offer to have a brief one-on-one conversation with each party to debrief. In these conversations, the mediator hopes to learn what that person thinks went well in the first session and how the mediator might set up a more productive second session with respect to substance (i.e., which topics are up for discussion) or format (i.e., how much time parties spend in joint session versus private session, how the mediator handles interruptions, etc.). These conversations are typically shorter than the initial pre-mediation conversations, on average about 30 minutes.

Goals of a second mediation session might be to continue to support the parties' productive communication and any of the following:

- Check on implementation of any agreements that came out of the first session.
- Possibly adapt agreements from the first session, based on how things have been working in practice.
- Explore additional topics or issues of concern raised by one or both parties.

Additional session(s)

Developing new habits can be difficult, so additional sessions may be helpful to support the parties as they work on new ways to interact. Just as before, offering a brief one-on-one meeting with each party before a subsequent session can be a good way to do another check-in, to find out how things are going and what would be most helpful to explore in an additional mediation session. Not all parties will take up the mediator's invitation for a check-in conversation, but just extending the invitation will telegraph to people that getting a working relationship back on track almost always takes time, patience, and a willingness to try new things, and that the mediator is available to provide support along the way.

What is a caucus session? What happens in them and why are they used?

Most mediators use the process option of a caucus, or private one-on-one meeting with a party, during a mediation session. (Some mediators practice a "no caucus" mediation model, which will be described in Chapter 9 as it relates to mediator styles and selection.) The one-on-one nature of the private caucus allows the mediator to build trust and rapport with a party. In caucus, without the other party present, the mediator can be fully attuned to the needs of one party, listening closely and responding to the party's substantive and emotional interests. In *Ripples from Peace Lake: Essays for Mediators and Peacemakers*, mediator Eric Galton describes this opportunity as "the most intimate, direct interaction between the mediator and a party,"[1] especially if the two have not had the opportunity to meet first in a pre-mediation conversation.

Another benefit of the caucus format is for the mediator to serve in the role of neutral negotiation coach, assisting each party in understanding their own interests and how best to convey their interests and ideas for moving forward to the other side. A mediator may also

1. Eric Galton, Ripples from Peace Lake: Essays for Mediators and Peacemakers 30 (2006).

opt for caucusing with parties individually for other reasons. Mediator David Hoffman, in his article "Mediation and the Art of Shuttle Diplomacy," argues that caucusing can help mediators overcome a variety of potential barriers—ones connected to communication, emotion, information, culture, among others. In workplace mediations involving a continuing relationship, the mediator might find that engaging in a round (or two) of caucus sessions, to address one or more such barriers before bringing parties back to a joint session, is productive. (For example, sometimes the information shared by parties with the mediator during the first round of caucusing has not yet been shared with the other party. If the parties agree to allow the mediator to share or "shuttle" new information back and forth, a second round of caucusing can give parties the space and time necessary to digest the new information and decide how it impacts their approach to the mediation.) The mediator, in consultation with the parties, can choose which process option, or sequence of options, is the right fit for the parties and conflict at hand.

What about virtual mediations?

How does mediating virtually compare to the in-person process? Do mediators have a preference? Are the outcomes the same?

COVID left many legacies, and as anyone who meets regularly with others knows very well, one of the biggest is that now people can get together and do business without ever leaving the office (or living room). Pre-pandemic, everyone expected to meet in person for mediation, because discussing sensitive information or topics virtually wasn't something most people welcomed. But Zoom and other virtual platforms have changed all that.

Do parties like and want online mediation? One helpful data point is a 2022 study by the Equal Employment Opportunity Commission (EEOC) on the topic that compared the experiences of in-person mediation participants in 2000 with those of virtual participants in 2021. In addition to finding that approximately 70 percent preferred online dispute resolution to in-person mediations, the EEOC also found that a higher percentage of parties (from both sides) were satisfied with their online dispute resolution results as compared to satisfaction rates with in-person mediation results.[2]

Mediators seem to agree. In a study of the experiences of 20 mediators who had mediated 1,000 Zoom mediations, mediator and Suffolk University emeritus law professor Dwight Golann found that many were pleasantly surprised by how well Zoom mediations had worked for them and their parties. "We like it much better than we thought we would" is the gist of what he heard.[3] In addition to savings in cost and time, mediators noted that parties, who were typically in the comfort of their own homes, seemed more relaxed in Zoom mediations. Moreover, both mediators and parties reflected on the impact of seeing their "self-view" in Zoom and making adjustments if they thought they looked angry, for example. Virtual mediations may never replace in-person mediations, but it's clear now that they offer a convenient option that works well for many.

---

2. *See* "The Equal Employment Opportunity Commission Mediation Participants Experience in Online Mediation and Comparison to In-Person Mediation," Equal Employment Opportunity Commission (Feb. 18, 2022), https://www.eeoc.gov/equal-employment-opportunity-commission-mediation-participants-experience-online-mediation-and.

3. Dwight Golann, *"I Sometimes Catch Myself Looking Angry or Tired. . .": The Impact of Mediating by Zoom*, 39 Alternatives to the High Cost of Litig. 1 (May 2021).

9

What's Involved in Selecting the Right Mediator for the Conflict?

There are several factors to consider when selecting a mediator:

- The mediator's subject matter expertise: Does this person specialize in certain kinds of cases—or is she more of a generalist?
- The mediator's experience: How long has he been mediating? Years? Decades? Months?
- How does the mediator describe her style? Labels mean different things to different practitioners and clients, but some common ones are facilitative, evaluative, and transformative.
- Where is the mediator based? If the mediation will be in-person, will she have to travel—and charge for that?
- How much does the mediator charge? What is the hourly fee and what is the estimate for mediation services for this case?

Other considerations can come into play, too. In a case involving allegations of race discrimination or bias, the department head who decides to seek outside help might think the mediator must be a person of color, someone with relevant lived experiences to bring to the mediation. This criterion assumes that the shared identity—race or ethnicity, for example—will mean that the mediator has life experiences similar to those of one of the parties, an assumption that may not always hold true. Sometimes searching for someone with relevant cultural experience, knowledge, or empathy about the primary issues can create a wider net and end with a good match.

Is there any research that provides guidance on when it might be helpful to factor in a mediator's race or gender in mediator selection? In their review of prior research, Indiana University professor Lisa Blomgren Amsler and colleagues Alexander B. Avtgis and M. Scott Jackman note that the "empirical work on demographics in mediation varies widely in research design and has produced mixed results."[1] Their own 2017 study of hundreds of mediations in the U.S. Postal Service REDRESS (Resolve Employment Disputes, Reach Equitable Solutions Swiftly) employment discrimination mediation program examined the impact of a complainant having the same race or gender as the mediator in a discrimination case. They found that African American complainants were equally satisfied with the mediation process and mediators in race discrimination cases, regardless of the mediator's race (though less satisfied about the outcome). Regarding gender, the study found that women complainants were equally satisfied with mediation process, mediators, and outcome in sex discrimination cases, regardless of the mediator's gender.[2]

A 2010 study, however, found different results on identity matching based on examining the experience of a party who does *not* share the same race or gender as the mediator. In their empirical study of 70 community or court-program mediations, mediators and University of Baltimore professors Lorig Charkoudian and Ellen Kabcenell Wayne found that while matching race or ethnicity did not have as much of an impact as they anticipated, there was a negative impact on "isolated" parties, those who did not share the same race or ethnicity of the mediator and the opposing party. More specifically, the isolated party was "less likely to perceive the mediator as listening without judgment" and "felt less control over the conflict" at the end of the mediation as compared to the start of the process.[3] The authors link this conclusion, perhaps in a

1. Lisa Blomgren Amsler, Alexander B. Avtgis & M. Scott Jackman, *Dispute System Design and Bias in Dispute Resolution*, 70 SMU L. Rev. 913, 931 (2017).
2. *Id.* at 939.
3. Lorig Charkoudian & Ellen Kabcenell Wayne, *Fairness, Understanding, and Satisfaction: Impact of Mediator and Participant Race and Gender on Participants' Perception of Mediation*, Conflict Resol. Q. 23, 45 (2010).

counterintuitive way, to the concern that using "demographic categories oversimplifies the concept of group identification. People who belong to the same racial or ethnic group will likely be aware of the extent of intra-group diversity and therefore recognize when they have little in common with a same-group mediator. A participant who does not belong to this identity group, however, may oversimplify and see the other's group as culturally monolithic and consistent. Facing two people linked by perceived commonalities she lacks, the participant may feel isolated in the mediation."[4] They conclude that using co-mediation and matching race or ethnicity of mediators with parties (a practice common in community mediation programs, when possible) or avoiding matching identities altogether could be helpful options.

Contrary to the U.S. Postal Service REDRESS mediation study, this study found that the gender of the mediator had an impact on how a mediation party perceived the mediator's fairness. The researchers found that when there was no gender match between party and mediator, the mediation party perceived the mediator as being unfair (i.e., perceived them as being judgmental, taking sides, etc.). This perceived bias effect worsened if a mediation party was isolated—if the gender of the mediator matched the opposing party only. Finally, the study found that parties whose gender did not match the mediator were also less satisfied with the mediation process. As a result, the authors support efforts to match mediation participants and mediators by gender when possible.[5]

In closing, while these studies offer additional data points on mediator selection, given the variation in study design and findings, they should be taken as only one potential factor to consider in the process of identifying a workplace mediator. The preceding discussion may also demonstrate how it is helpful to approach each mediation with fresh eyes to determine what qualities are needed in a mediator for that specific conflict; in some instances, inviting parties' input in the process may be a productive first step. (More on this in the Mediator Selection Process section later in the chapter.)

---

4. *Id.*
5. *Id.* at 44.

Mediator styles

In addition to considering a mediator's subject matter expertise and other qualifications, the individual identifying the mediator should also consider two process-related points: (1) the style of the mediator and (2) the process of mediator selection. Most mediators have a primary style, typically divided into two common types, facilitative and evaluative. (A third type, transformative, which focuses on the parties' relationship and their empowerment, is less common today, but has been used in the highly regarded U.S. Postal Service workplace mediation program, REDRESS.)

On a practical level, the mediator's style will affect who comes up with ideas for how to resolve the conflict. A facilitative mediator, for example, will work to assist the parties in identifying their needs and interests and in developing options to satisfy the parties' interests—but generally won't make suggestions for resolution. By contrast, an evaluative mediator usually is comfortable making recommendations to the parties and perhaps providing predictions about what might happen if the case moved to court or an administrative proceeding. Because many retired judges describe themselves as evaluative mediators, here's another way to think about this: If you're looking for a mediator who will be willing to discuss the chances your argument will prevail in court, consider an evaluative mediator who spent years hearing cases and handing down decisions.

Another mediator style question relates to the use of caucus. Some mediators have a strong preference about the use of caucus—whether they should be used always or never. As discussed earlier in Chapter 8, many or even most mediators use caucus as a process option in mediation, with some mediating exclusively or primarily in caucus sessions. Mediators Gary Friedman, Jack Himmelstein, and Robert Mnookin, however, champion the "no-caucus" or understanding-based model for mediations. As outlined in their book, *Challenging Conflict: Mediation Through Understanding*, Friedman and Himmelstein believe that the power of understanding should drive the process and that the parties themselves should work directly together to take responsibility for the dispute and the resolution.

While there are distinctions between styles, Northwestern law professor Len Riskin reminds us in his seminal articles on this topic that most mediators exhibit more than one style in their practice, even within a single mediation, in response to the dynamics of the case. Still, because there are differences in mediator style and approach, many of them nuanced, learning as much as possible about any one practitioner (through direct conversation or anecdotally) is always wise.

Mediator selection process

A brief example might help illustrate the importance of thinking through the decision-making process for mediator selection—and including parties' input in some way.

HOW MUCH SAY SHOULD PARTIES HAVE? IT'S COMPLICATED.

An HR director reaches out to Jeremy, a mediator who is Jewish, after a Jewish educator named Avi accused the school administrator Theo of making anti-Jewish remarks. Can Jeremy help? Jeremy is interested in the case, but knowing that mediations involving identity can be especially challenging and complicated, he suggests that the employer compile a list of three mediators and let the parties have a voice in the selection. Along with the HR director, Avi and Theo could look over the mediators' bios, talk briefly with each one to learn more about their background and experiences, and weigh in. The parties agree to this, and both say they're grateful for the chance to help choose.

Avi, Theo, and the HR director eventually agree on Jeremy, and he begins his usual pre-mediation conversations with Theo, the colleague accused of making anti-Jewish remarks. In that discussion, Theo tells the mediator that his friends all urged him not to pick Jeremy, who, they said, would surely be biased in favor of the Jewish coworker. But Theo said he responded indignantly. "Why shouldn't I choose him?" he asked his friends. "He's clearly the most qualified."

(continued)

(continued)

> But then Theo makes a small confession to Jeremy: When asked to rank the mediator candidates, he selected one of the other mediators as his top choice. Why? He knew Avi would rank Jeremy #1, and Theo definitely didn't want Avi to have his way.

Bottom line—parties care about the mediator they will work with—and about the process of choosing that mediator. For some cases, it might be useful for the employer contact to provide potential parties with a panel of mediators to consider and rank in order of preference. As part of that initial process, the parties might ask for a brief informational meeting with each mediator so the mediator can introduce himself and answer questions about his background, experiences, and approach. Giving the parties input into the process of choosing a mediator, when possible, can be a key step in getting their buy-in for the process itself.

10

What Is an Agreement to Mediate?

Whether the case is in small claims court or a private mediation, before the mediation begins, mediators give parties an all-important document to review and sign. The wording of Agreements to Mediate vary (and some may be more technical than others), but they are all generally designed to explain the process of mediation, let parties know about its limitations and possibilities, and describe how the mediator will approach the process. Topics include the following:

- An overview of the mediation process
- The role of the mediator
- Voluntariness
- Confidentiality
- Disclosure of prior relationships or possible conflicts of interest
- Mediation fees

In workplace mediations, the individual participating parties typically sign the Agreement. An organizational representative may sign in connection with the fee, or that can be addressed in a separate memo between the mediator and the person financially responsible.

What if I have questions about the Agreement? Do I need a lawyer to review the Agreement with me?

The mediator, or someone in that person's office, is typically available to answer parties' questions about the Agreement, and most mediators are happy to explain the wording and discuss its content to ensure the parties fully understand and agree to it before starting work together. But because impartiality is an important component of the mediator's role, the mediator (and any member of the mediator's firm) cannot ethically give advice about signing the Agreement. If parties have concerns or need guidance, most mediators will encourage them to consult an attorney.

What if a party wants to make changes to the Agreement?

Some aspects of the Agreement (such as confidentiality, for example) can't usually be deleted or changed substantially, but most often parties can adapt the Agreement in other ways to suit their needs. The catch is that both parties and the mediator must agree to the proposed changes. It may sound unlikely, but it can happen.

WHAT'S CONFIDENTIAL?

After reviewing the Agreement, Jina, a party in a workplace mediation, asks the mediator about making two substantive changes.

Since she and her coworker at a local senior center had a very public shouting match several months back, Jina has found the tension at work extremely stressful. Talking with her brother, who is a professor at an upstate college, however, has been a big help, she says, and she wonders about a carve-out that would let her continue these conversations. Because Jina's brother works far from the nonprofit and has no connections to that community or town, the other party in the case, her coworker Shaheen, is comfortable agreeing with the suggested change.

Also, because Shaheen is a supervisor, Jina asks for language specifying that what is said in mediation will not find its way into any performance reviews or disciplinary steps. Shaheen has some hesitations about this request, not knowing exactly what might be said, but she's interested in trying to improve the working relationship and so agrees to the change.

As the exchanges between Jina and Shaheen show, reviewing and discussing the Agreement is much more than just an administrative step: It's actually the start of the mediation. And reaching agreement on wording can be a great beginning for discussing the more challenging topics that have brought parties to mediation in the first place.

Can the process start before the Agreement is signed?

Ideally, the parties and mediator will review and sign the Agreement before any substantive discussions begin. That being said, in some instances, initial conversations, such as pre-mediation calls, can happen before signing, as long as the delay in signing is a technicality—if, for example, someone has reviewed it and is ready to sign but has no access to a printer and no ability to sign electronically. In other cases, the formal protections of a signed Agreement may be necessary or wise (perhaps there is concern about one party maintaining confidentiality, given prior statements to others in the community or on social media), and the mediator will choose to wait for everyone to sign before getting to work.

11

What Is a Conflicts Check? Why Is It Necessary?

Knowing that the mediator's impartiality is a core principle of mediation, mediators take time to ensure that no conflict of interest, real or perceived, might interfere with their ability to work on specific cases. This is called a conflicts check, and it's an important way to ensure that parties feel comfortable that the person they're working with has no past or current connections to either party that could make the mediator biased—or create the appearance of favoritism.

Many mediators maintain a searchable database or system to check the names of mediation parties and interested parties against past clients of the firm, for mediation or other services. While the approach may vary, each mediator should have a method to meet this objective, even if it is simply to have an extensive conversation with parties at the outset to try to determine, to everyone's satisfaction, that no conflicts exist. In most instances, a conflicts check yields no information that would preclude a mediator from serving in a case, but sometimes there might be a need for a disclosure to parties before proceeding.

What kind of potential conflict of interest might require disclosure? The simplest kinds of conflicts are those that involve the parties (or their extended family members) and the mediator directly, such as the mediator having worked with one of the parties in a previous mediation. In those cases, the answer is clear: Disclosure of the past work together is required. (Perhaps ironically, sometimes cases come to mediators precisely because the mediator *has* worked with one side before; somewhat counterintuitively, the side that has not worked with the "repeat" mediator is often thrilled to work with "the other side's mediator" because they believe the mediator can "talk some sense" into the other party and resolve the intractable conflict.)

But what if the connection is less direct? What happens if the mediator is a member of a firm, and a colleague there once mediated another conflict involving one of the parties? Is that a problem? The mediator should err on the side of disclosure, telling both parties that a colleague at the firm has mediated a case involving one party in an unrelated matter. Once the information about the mediator's colleague's work is out, if everyone still wants to use the selected mediator, the mediation can continue.

What if the earlier dispute was not a mediation, but a court case that was successfully litigated by a colleague of the mediator? In this instance, because the past relationship was in an adverse action, litigation, simple disclosure isn't enough. The mediator might reach out to the prospective mediation client who was involved in the case and ask for permission to let the other party in the mediation know about it—and if so, how much detail the mediator can share. If the answer is yes and the other party has no objection, the mediator should consider drafting a Conflict of Interest Waiver, noting that one party was represented by the mediator's colleague in a prior unrelated matter (or was the opposing party in the previous case) and that both parties are comfortable proceeding. If both parties agree and sign the waiver, the mediation can continue.

Discussing possible conflicts, like reviewing the Agreement to Mediate, might sound administrative, but this is a key step to ensure that everyone in the mediation, including the mediator, is comfortable and confident that the mediator can be objective. Even when a conflict of interest surfaces later (as it sometimes does, when a party or mediator suddenly recognizes a connection), the only way to allay concern—or decide to stop the process and find another mediator—is to talk things through and make sure everyone understands and is OK to proceed.

12

What Are Pre-Mediation Calls or Pre-Mediation Submissions?

To help prepare for a mediation, both in terms of learning the substantive background and personality dynamics of the parties, mediators will often schedule pre-mediation phone or Zoom calls. In some cases, workplace mediators may also request pre-mediation written memos or submissions from the parties or their attorneys. (Attorneys do sometimes participate in workplace mediations, but because most workplace mediations involve only the neutral and the parties, I'm focusing here on those two-party cases. The next section deals with cases involving lawyers.)

Pre-mediation discussions—like the one in which the mediator learned that one party wanted to adapt the Agreement to confide in her brother or the case when one party had ranked the mediator at the bottom of a list of candidates—almost always provide helpful information. They also increase trust and the chance of settlement in employment disputes. A 2006 field study of 540 employment disputes by leadership and conflict resolution professor Roderick Swaab, of graduate business school INSEAD, found that mediators who use pre-mediation caucuses for the purpose of building trust—not to solve the substantive conflict—increase the likelihood of resolving the dispute.

Pre-mediation conversations are confidential. They fall within the confidentiality provisions of the entire mediation as described in the Agreement to Mediate and usually last less than an hour. In a pre-mediation conversation, a mediator may have the following goals in mind:

- Introduce herself by talking about her background and approach to mediation.
- Share information and answer questions about the mediation process.
- Review information from the Agreement to Mediate, as needed.
- Reiterate the confidentiality of one-on-one conversations and the mediation session(s).
- Learn about the party's perspective and experiences of the underlying conflict.
- Discuss the person's goals and interests for the mediation.
- Talk about what the mediator can do for this person to encourage full participation and engagement (i.e., how to handle interruptions, breaks, private caucus conversations, outbursts, or other matters).

Taking time in pre-mediation conversations to demystify the mediation process is important. In a 2007 study using data from 50 mediations between supervisors and direct reports in the Netherlands, researchers Katalien Bollen of the University of Leuven, Martin Euwema, a University of Leuven professor, and Patrick Müller of the University of Mannheim found that when subordinates experienced uncertainty about the mediation, their satisfaction with the mediation decreased. Given this, the authors recommend that mediators make conscious efforts to minimize the uncertainty a subordinate party might experience in mediation by providing thorough and specific information about the mediation process, the role of the mediator, and possible outcomes. Because subordinates may have more uncertainty than supervisors about the process, one-on-one pre-mediation conversations are probably the best way for the mediator to help allay concerns. Supervisors' concerns deserve equal attention, of course, but most bosses probably will approach the process with less anxiety than those they supervise.

Are lawyers ever involved?

Some workplace mediations do include attorneys or counsel. Perhaps one side has announced that he has hired a lawyer and will file a complaint if the mediation is not successful, and the other party, hearing this, has also retained counsel. In these instances, in the pre-mediation calls, the mediator will probably talk only to the attorneys, who typically prefer to handle such communications themselves. Those conversations usually cover the topics listed earlier, but the mediator might also want to find out what each lawyer's experience has been with the other party's lawyer (which is why many mediators talk with lawyers separately). Have past interactions been constructive? Contentious because of some other, unresolved matter? Any and all information will help the mediator prepare and be ready for difficult dynamics between the parties or even the lawyers.

If attorneys participate in the actual mediation, many mediators are careful to make sure the parties know that the parties, not their lawyers, are the ones with the power to decide what happens in mediation. For example, if a mediator invites each side to share its goals for the mediation session and counsel for one side speaks first, the mediator may then invite that lawyer's client to add to or clarify the attorney's remarks. And many times they do, especially in private sessions.

Will the mediator speak to anyone other than the parties (or their attorneys)?

The quick answer for many cases is no—but sometimes mediators will end up speaking to others, particularly during intake conversations. For example, the employer contact who initially reached out to the mediator—an HR manager, a department head, or even general counsel—will usually share some background information with the mediator to explain the conflict and determine whether mediation is the right process and the mediator is the right person for the job. In these conversations, the employer contact may share information that will help the mediator understand the context of the conflict, how the dispute is affecting others, or how one or both parties are perceived. This kind of initial background conversation—gathered in an intake conversation or in a separate conversation—is confidential, and the mediator won't disclose its content to the participating parties or anyone outside the mediation.

Will parties provide any written information or documents to the mediator before the mediation?

Information from pre-mediation calls can sometimes make a mediator want to know more about a document or communication: Perhaps an email that triggered a shouting match, or a performance review that the employee has strong objections to. In this sense, there may be "submissions" to the mediator, but these are much more organic than the pre-mediation submissions, such as memos and copies of a complaint, that lawyers in traditional mediations for cases in litigation often supply. (One note: In the case of an email or performance review, some mediators may choose *not* to review the actual document but instead invite the party who mentioned it to describe it and explain what it means to them. This way, the mediator learns the significance of the document to the party and their perception of it. It also helps distinguish mediation from litigation, in which documents are reviewed as evidence. And in many instances, what might really matter is the party's interpretation of the email or review—not the mediator's impression of it.)

13

If I'm a Party in a Workplace Mediation, How Should I Prepare?

Some mediators share "prep questions" with parties, either in writing or in their pre-mediation conversations. These are often focused on interest-based negotiation, with the goal of eliciting a party's needs and interests and asking the person to reflect on what they care about most. (As the earlier scenarios showed, interests in workplace cases vary, but many involve concerns about reputation, job security, or transparency.) Another prep question might be designed to get the party thinking about options for resolution or possible terms of an agreement, and, importantly, options that the other side might also see as beneficial (or beneficial enough). A final prep question might be for the party to consider what will happen if they don't reach a satisfactory agreement in the mediation: What is their BATMA, or Best Alternative to a Mediated Agreement? Is the status quo sustainable? Are things so bad that if the situation continues, the party might think about quitting? Or is that not a possibility because they don't have another job lined up?

These are questions common for any mediation preparation. Still others may be helpful in getting parties to think ahead and be reflective for a workplace mediation. For example:

- What might happen in the mediation to make you feel it was a good use of your time?
- What's one thing you'd like to learn in this process?
- What's one thing the other person doesn't know now that might be helpful for them to learn—and is something you're open to talking about?
- How might your past experiences be influencing how you are seeing the current conflict and the other person?
- What topics do you want to explore in mediation? Any subjects you don't want to discuss?
- What one thing (or two or three things) can the mediator do to help you participate fully? Is there some part of the process, as described by the mediator or in the Agreement to Mediate, that you especially welcome or worry about?

Asking a party to reflect on these pre-mediation questions beforehand can lead to a productive dialogue in mediation. Reflection, an exercise crucial to constructive and effective dialogue, can help someone step back and break a cycle of reacting, which can prolong and deepen tension between two people who aren't getting along.

In her research on how to apply dialogic concepts to classroom teaching and dispute resolution, Southern Methodist University religious studies professor Jill DeTemple argues that dialogic practices, such as inviting time for reflection, can shift a contentious space to one in which relationships "allow connection across differences in worldview and/or experience."[1]

Psychologist Corky Becker describes reflection as "the act of looking at your thoughts and feelings and deciding intentionally how you want to respond to your thoughts and feelings. . . . Reacting is when feelings drive what you want to say. . . . If feelings are driving what you want to say, and you're threatened, you might be driven to say things in anger and fear, or hide out and freeze, for example, and not in a constructive way. In reflection, you're stopping, you're thinking, you're deciding intentionally how you want to put together all your feelings in connection with what

1. Jill DeTemple, *The Spaces We Make: Dialogic Classrooms and Social Transformation*, Ohio St. J. on Disp. Resol. 753, 777 (2020).

you care about and who you want to be, how you want to be and how you want to come across" to another person.[2]

In other words, when a party takes time to consider what they would like to discuss—and how—*before* the mediation, they will often feel more ready and confident to do so in the mediation. As DeTemple and her co-authors Harriett Hayes of Bridgewater College and Jennifer Ellis West of Samford University explain in *The Dialogic Classroom in Higher Education*, this is especially true for people for whom English is not their first language, internal processors, or those who might not be confident speaking in front of others. Reflecting gives people more agency, allowing them to choose what part of their experience they want to share with the other party. (The mediator can also help coach a party, before or in the mediation, on how they'd like to convey certain information, experiences, or perspectives.) And after reflection, many people will be better able to listen and learn.

2. Robert R. Stains, Jr., *Reflection for Connection: Deepening Dialogue Through Reflective Processes*, Conflict Resol. Q. 33, 38–39 (2012).

In the Mediation: Managing Parties and the Process

14

What's a Typical Agenda for the Mediation Session?

As described in Chapter 12, during their pre-mediation conversations, mediators usually give parties a sense of what to expect in the mediation session, most often describing the mediation process and topics that are likely to come up.

During the initial joint session, some mediators invite the parties to talk about the questions the mediator provided in advance: What would a party consider a good use of their time? What would they like to learn from the session or sessions? . . . and other questions designed to jump-start parties' thinking. Other topics for a first session might include:

- What drew each of you to the work you're doing?
- What is something you love about your work? (With this, the mediator is essentially urging the parties to think on the positive side—and ideally realize that resolving differences will allow them to focus more time and energy on something they enjoy.)
- What would each of you like to see happen going forward?
- How could trust be rebuilt between the two of you?

- How do you like people to communicate with you (i.e., in person? by phone? Skype, Slack, etc.)?
- Can you think of one idea for improving communication between the two of you?
- If you have a difference of opinion in the future, how would you like the other person to discuss it with you? What would you *not* like them to do?

With these questions and others like them, the mediator hopes to encourage each of the people involved to start talking about their experiences, perspectives, and hopes—and to hear the other person talk about the same things. Mediators might think of an opening question or two, to get the conversation started, but many take their cues from the parties, who often bring up topics or questions they want to spend time discussing.

Workplace mediation agendas focus on how to improve people's relationship in the workplace. Some coworkers have never been—and don't want to be—close friends or allies, while others might really want to restore what once was a great connection. But in every conflict, unless one or both are prepared to leave the job, most people understand at some point in the process that if they want to get work done, they'll have to figure out how to interact in a respectful, collaborative way.

With this as a general end goal, most workplace mediations follow this roadmap:

Mediator's opening
The mediator welcomes the parties and provides a brief overview of the process, touching on some points from the Agreement to Mediate including goals, roles, confidentiality, voluntariness, and process options, including the possibility of the mediator meeting with each party in private sessions or caucuses.

Initial joint session—initial exchanges
After the opening, the mediator, reminding the parties about the pre-mediation questions designed to prompt reflection, may invite the parties to talk about what they'd like to accomplish in mediation.

Private sessions

Many mediators use private caucuses, one-on-one meetings with each party, as a chance to get real-time feedback on what's been happening and what that person would like to talk about in joint sessions. With proper preview in the opening remarks, parties will know that this will be a way to ensure that everyone is comfortable and fully able to participate. In the private sessions, most mediators will take care to explain an extra layer of confidentiality—and clarify what information from those sessions, if any, the party is willing to have the mediator repeat or bring up in joint session.

Additional joint session and exchanges

After a round of private sessions, the mediator may return to a joint session to discuss topics raised in the private session (with the permission of the parties), wrap up the conversation, or both. Here's where the idea of a follow-up session comes in: Even if it's unclear whether a later session will be needed, many parties like the idea of scheduling another meeting in which they can continue the conversation, discuss new topics, or reflect on what's been said or done. So the mediator may schedule a future mediation session with the parties and also let them know she will reach out for a one-on-one debrief or check-in conversation following the first mediation session. In that conversation, the mediator and party can discuss how things went in the mediation session and consider what would be helpful to explore in the subsequent mediation session.

Are private sessions really necessary? Isn't bringing people together and then speaking to each person privately counterproductive?

Perhaps the simplest way to address these questions is with an example.

MISSED CUES

Jamal is mediating discussions between Grace and Valentina, two colleagues in a pharmaceutical company who lead teams that are collaborating on the development of a new drug. Looking at their past performance, their supervisors expected these two talented women to be terrific collaborators, but ever since Valentina joined the firm several months ago, things have been rocky. The workplace has very tight deadlines and very high expectations, and Grace and Valentina's wildly different communication styles have increased the stress level considerably.

Valentina and Grace are both committed to their jobs, Jamal knows, and agree that their main task is to improve their communication. With this in mind, Jamal chooses to begin the first mediation session in joint session and keeps the two women together, encouraging them to think and talk about how they can communicate more productively.

In a follow-up debrief conversation with Valentina after the end of the first session, however, Jamal is surprised to hear that Valentina was immensely frustrated with how Grace behaved in that first session. Grace, Valentina said, never accepted any responsibility for her own actions and spent the entire time blaming and complaining about Valentina. Valentina couldn't figure out how to point this out in joint session without prompting another blowup.

Jamal realizes that a private caucus sometime during the first session, even just a brief one, would have given Valentina a chance to express her frustration, and Jamal could have course-corrected back in joint session. There's still time and hope, though: Jamal lets Valentina know that he'll keep her frustration in mind during the second session, and he urges Valentina to let him know if she needs a break before Jamal moves to private sessions the next time they meet.

Mediators are trained to listen for parties' spoken and unspoken needs; what's especially challenging, even for veteran mediators, can be *reading* their needs. Realities such as someone's habitual reluctance to speak up or disagree or a power imbalance between parties can make this task even more difficult. Checking in with each party before the mediation has progressed far, talking privately for at least a few minutes, can be a great way to make sure that unspoken needs and unvoiced emotions get addressed.

15

Is the Process Really Confidential?

As mentioned earlier, most workplace mediators are hired by someone inside an organization—often an HR official or department leader—after efforts to deal with things internally have failed. And the employer's the one who's paying the mediator. All this makes many parties wonder: Is workplace mediation *really* confidential?

One answer, briefly touched on in Chapter 6, is yes—to some extent. In initial conversations with the employer contact, most mediators will explain that to facilitate engagement and candor, mediation is a confidential process. What does that mean for these kinds of cases? Most often it means that the mediator will not report back anything substantive about what's said in mediation to the employer point of contact unless both parties agree that this is OK. The employer is usually eager to know about the general progress of things—that pre-mediation or initial sessions have been scheduled or held, for instance, or that parties and the mediator want to meet again—but what's discussed in the room almost always stays between the parties and the mediator. (One note: A difference in the work of an organizational ombuds and workplace mediator is related to reporting systemic issues. An ombuds, for example, identifies and shares systemic issues with the organization's leadership to build awareness about conflict patterns and help improve the overall climate of the organization, whereas the mediator is charged solely with assisting the two employees with their conflict.)

However, as discussed in Chapter 6, mediators may include a few exceptions to confidentiality in the Agreement to Mediate and review these exceptions with parties before beginning work. Common exceptions may include permitting, but not requiring, disclosure by the mediator or parties of information about the risk of serious harm to an individual or child or elder abuse or neglect. Whenever an exception to confidentiality seems wise, the mediator should explicitly confirm with the parties what information will be shared and why.

Even experienced mediators might not be able to anticipate all questions or concerns related to confidentially. Consider the following scenario:

FOR YOUR INFORMATION ONLY

(The mediation with senior center workers Jina and Shaheen, continued)

Jina has spoken up about wanting to confide in her brother and being concerned that statements in mediation might surface in future discipline or performance reviews. Once her supervisor Shaheen has agreed to these exceptions, Jina says she is worried about something else: that others at the senior center, a small place with several employees who like to gossip, will hear about the mediation and what it's about. How can Jina be sure that this mediation conversation will be just between her and Shaheen, with the mediator helping and contributing as needed?

> The mediator's answer is short and quick: She typically tells the employer contact—in this case, the center's HR manager—only process-related information such as the dates when mediation sessions have been scheduled and the date the work is done. But Jina is still worried. She bumped up against the HR manager in recent weeks, when the disagreement was heating up, and she doesn't trust him at all. Can the mediator restrict information-sharing to the center's director and its billing agency, which would be done through the mediator's invoices? The mediator proposes this to the HR manager, who has no objections. Everyone agrees, and the mediation proceeds.

This sort of detail might seem small, but it was crucial for Jina to feel comfortable with the mediation process.

16

Is It Really Voluntary?

If an employee is told to attend mediation, is it really voluntary? Some parties may simply ask the mediator directly, while others will share up front that they felt compelled to participate in mediation because they feared some kind of retribution—disciplinary action, informal or formal, or even dismissal.

In response, most mediators acknowledge that although parties might not be at the table by their own choice (and probably have been strongly urged or even required to participate), what actually happens in the mediation—what's discussed and whatever agreements may arise—is entirely in the parties' hands.

There are degrees of voluntariness, and finding out where parties fit on that scale early on can be helpful. If participation was ordered or is required to avoid some other action (such as discipline), the mediator's explanation of content control will be especially important. Imagine the following scenario: A company director overseeing two talented but bickering trainees makes participation in mediation a requirement for consideration for a full-time job at the company. The director's rationale is that the two will continue working together going forward if they both accept job offers, which are likely to be extended, and he thinks they need to resolve their conflict before taking on permanent positions at the company.

Here, it's clear the parties did not choose mediation on their own. In addition to talking with the employer contact about the importance of voluntariness, the mediator can emphasize to the contact and the parties that how the time is used, and any agreements coming from it, are completely within the hands of the two parties—not the employer contact. After discussing this with the parties, if the mediator does not feel comfortable with the level of voluntariness, she could let the employer contact know she is not able to proceed with the mediation.

Even if someone is in mediation voluntarily, they may be uncomfortable. Or upset or even angry about the underlying conflict, and their emotions may leak into how they interact with the mediator. Part of the mediator's job—in the initial intake or pre-mediation conversations—is to get a sense for what might still be keeping someone from participating in mediation with an open mind and a willingness to listen.

In mediation training, trainers often say that if the mediator is working harder than the parties, that's a problem—the idea being that the parties are the ones who should do the hard work involved in listening, talking, and brainstorming ideas for resolution. At this point, that warning might extend to how hard the mediator is trying to "sell" mediation to a party; ideally, mediators should not be in the business of giving people a "hard sell" about mediation simply to convince them to participate. Instead, mediators can and should share information and answer questions (about process, the mediator's style, and other matters), but the question of whether to give mediation a try should be up to each party, knowing that each can choose to end the process at any time.

Understanding this—reframing the "selling" of the process, in other words—is an important step toward working to ensure that mediation is the right fit for any given party at any given moment.

17

Do the People Involved Need Lawyers or Other Advisors (Such as Union Reps)?

If people have heard about workplace mediation, they often think it's a last-ditch alternative to litigation or grievance procedures, a stop on the way to the courthouse or an EEO investigation. As discussed in Chapter 12, however, in most workplace cases, lawyers or other advisors are not involved in the actual mediation. They might be on the sidelines, advising parties in cases where someone is considering legal action or preparing for other more formal processes, but usually the people involved in a disagreement are the only ones at the mediation table, from start to finish.

But what if an employee is a member of a union? What is the role of the union in workplace mediations? In short, the answer depends on the specific collective bargaining agreement of the workplace, whether the mediation involves disciplinary issues, and, possibly, whether the state has adopted the Uniform Mediation Act (discussed in Chapter 6).

As noted earlier, the ideal time for workplace mediation is before any disciplinary action, and the focus of this book is on those earlier mediations. At the same time, because the line between disciplinary and non-disciplinary issues can be fuzzy, it's helpful to keep in mind how workplace mediation may intersect with the disciplinary process, here with the added wrinkle of union membership.

If an employee requests union representation in the mediation, that request should generally be honored for a few reasons. For example, if one or both employees reasonably believe that disciplinary issues may result, the employees have "Weingarten rights," or the right to union representation during an investigatory interview that could lead to discipline. (Weingarten rights were established by the U.S. Supreme Court in *NLRB v. J. Weingarten, Inc.* (1975), when it found that section 7 of the National Labor Relations Act provides this protection for union-represented employees who request it.) For many typical workplace mediations dealing with interpersonal dynamics and tensions, disciplinary issues, and therefore Weingarten rights, would not apply. However, even if an employee doesn't have a concern about possible discipline, the employee may still have a right to have a union representative attend the mediation, because some collective bargaining agreements specifically include language calling for union representation in non-disciplinary matters or because the conflict might fall under other terms covered by the bargaining agreement. (Because each bargaining agreement is unique, mediators may find it helpful to review a company's agreement beforehand, perhaps as a pre-mediation submission, and parties should consult their union rep with any questions.)

Even if a conflict does not fall within the workplace's bargaining agreement, a party might still be entitled to bring a union rep to mediation. Why? The state in question may have adopted language to this effect, as Connecticut recently did when it became the thirteenth state to adopt the UMA, effective October 1, 2025. Based on section 10 of the UMA passed in Connecticut, an "attorney or other individual designated by a party," such as a union rep, may accompany a party and participate in mediation.

As with any question or concern a party raises, learning more about what's driving a party's request for a union rep or other individual to attend the mediation will almost certainly be useful. Is it because the union rep could bring more experience, either as a negotiator or as someone who has seen a number of prior conflicts resolve in this workplace? Or is it because the party making the request would like to have a support person in the room? Perhaps the party feels uncomfortable with the process and if so, could the mediator answer questions to address the unknowns or concerns? Or does the party fear the mediation is the start of a disciplinary process?

If the last consideration is driving the request for a union rep to attend, the mediator will do well to clarify a few things. First, if the mediation is not related to discipline, the mediator and the referring employer contact will want to clarify this for the employee—and if discipline is not involved, the employee's Weingarten rights are not applicable. Second, in the mediation process, it's critical for a party to speak for herself; if she's not comfortable doing so, the mediator can usually help by providing more structure, for example, or sharing discussion questions in advance. Finally, given the confidentiality of the process as outlined in the Agreement to Mediate, everyone should be aware that matters discussed in the mediation process should not be disclosed to others outside the mediation, including for potential disciplinary purposes.

Last note: If someone other than the parties, such as a union rep, does attend the mediation, that person will have to agree to the mediation's confidentiality—and probably sign the Agreement to Mediate. The mediator will also want to let the other party know that a union rep will be attending so they can come prepared to speak to both the other party and union rep, consider bringing an additional person to even out the number of participants, or make other arrangements.

18

What Exactly Is the Mediator's Role?

Most mediators say their role is to impartially facilitate understanding, negotiation, and/or agreement between mediation parties. This notion of impartiality relates to the mediator's treatment of the parties—in simplest terms, the mediators shouldn't take sides in the conflict—as well as the substance of what the parties might agree to at the end of the process, meaning the mediator should not have a stake in the outcome. (Some mediators, such as Ken Cloke, take issue with the notion of impartiality and argue that mediators should actually be "omni-partial," or on the side of each party at all times.)

This description of mediation is in line with how most mediators describe mediation as a process: facilitated or assisted negotiation. While some mediators of more traditional cases might be evaluative, sharing opinions or possible solutions or predicting the outcome of a mediation case if it proceeds to trial, most mediators of early workplace conflicts would probably describe themselves as facilitative.

Will the mediator weigh in and help us decide what to do?

But will a facilitative mediator ever share ideas for how to resolve the conflict? Even after the mediator has explained her role as a neutral facilitator, parties may still expect (or hope) that the mediator will provide substantive guidance such as recommendations for how to move forward. Sometimes the easiest way to address this expectation is to talk about what would happen if the mediator did make suggestions. For example, what if she recommended that in their agreement the parties include a requirement that they each take notes at their meetings and exchange them afterward to help ensure both are on the same page regarding next steps? Fast forward to the next day or week. One of the employees involved hates the idea of writing everything down, and upon reflection thinks that this benefits only the other employee, who always keeps detailed notes. The employee who hates taking notes decides to give up—and rips up the agreement. The employee who likes the comfort of a written record then claims that the coworker is in violation of the agreement.

This kind of outcome is one reason most mediators shy away from giving parties substantive advice or suggestions. Parties who craft their own understandings or agreements, using their own words and their own ideas, are more likely to abide by those agreements and consider the mediation a success. That being said, if parties get stuck or draw a blank, some mediators will ask whether the parties would like to hear how other parties have addressed similar issues, and if everyone is interested, will share a few ideas that have worked for others. The line between sharing past practices and recommending or advocating for solutions is a fine but often crucial one.

What if the parties want to participate in coaching because mediation sounds like the conflict is headed to court? As noted several times before, in the minds of many people, especially those who have never been involved in the process or known someone who has, mediation means litigation might be right around the corner. So if semantics is a problem, should mediators simply call their work coaching, which for many brings to mind good things like self-improvement and support? Consider the following scenario:

COACH OR MEDIATOR?

HR director Tyrone is concerned that his employees will not want to try mediation because it sounds like a legal process. So Tyrone asks the mediator, Zaineb, if she could frame the work as "team coaching," with the mediator serving as coach. Zaineb agrees to this, but in the mediation itself she describes her role as that of a facilitative mediator and conducts the first session as she would any other workplace mediation.

After that session, the parties decide not to schedule a second meeting. In a wrap-up email to them, Zaineb offers a quick debrief conversation to each person and is pleased to hear back from one of the parties, Becca. In that conversation, Becca tells Zaineb that even though Zaineb clearly defined her role as facilitative, Becca was disappointed and frustrated because she wanted and expected the coach to provide more guidance and ideas to help the team of two move forward.

While coaching has great benefits and can be hugely helpful, especially for someone looking for individual advice and attention focused on growth and improvement, it's not mediation. So mediators and the people they seek to help should be clear about what the mediation process is—and what everyone should expect from it. As with questions about bias and confidentiality, clear explanations about the process and roles are always important.

Finally, part of the mediator's role may have to do with offering a calm, impartial presence for the parties to work through their conflict. In their book, *Bringing Peace into the Room*, mediators Daniel Bowling and David Hoffman write about how the personal qualities of the mediator, the "psychological, intellectual and spiritual qualities that make a person who he or she is," impact the process and outcome of mediations.[1] In

1. Daniel Bowling & David Hoffman, Bringing Peace into the Room: How the Personal Qualities of the Mediator Impact the Process of Conflict Resolution 14 (2003).

short, they reflect on the fact that when they, as mediators, have been at peace with themselves and the world, they have been better able to bring peace into the room and positively influence the mediation. Bowling and Hoffman also see the source of the mediator's influence (or a component of her role) as drawing from the "Hawthorne effect," a social science term for the changes people make in their behavior when they know they are being observed. While mediators do far more than merely observe parties in mediation, considering this aspect of their presence can be instructive.

Will the mediator be actively involved the whole time—or will the parties sometimes directly engage in conversation themselves?

The mediator is typically more involved in facilitating conversation between the parties at the outset of the mediation, and if those present are tracking speaking time, the mediator will probably have the most lines, at least to start. But after an opening and welcome, the mediator may turn to one of the prep questions she sent the parties beforehand, or she may invite parties to share agenda items or topics they'd like to explore. Whatever subject comes up first, good mediators will pay close attention to both parties in these opening minutes, watching and listening to gauge each party's comfort level, reactions, and emotions.

What does this early stage look like? One example: The mediator may choose a question and invite each party to answer, taking time between responses to repeat back, or paraphrase, what's been said. This reflective, or active, listening has several advantages. Summarizing what he thinks he has heard can help a mediator be sure that he's got it right—and allows the person who spoke to make corrections or additions on the spot as needed. Repeating aloud what one party has said, even using the same (or similar) words and relaying the same message, also lets the other person at the table hear those words and that message in the mediator's voice, not the other party's. Perhaps because they have become so entangled with the other person, people in conflict often find words easier to hear—and contemplate—when they're delivered by a neutral, someone with whom they have no history and no intractable disagreement.

Mediators can also facilitate negotiations between the parties, and as noted elsewhere, many neutrals find private meetings, or caucuses, especially useful for moving along negotiations or discussions. In joint session, mediators attend to the dynamic at the table, but in caucus sessions, the mediator can turn her attention to the individual party and serve as an impartial coach, helping each party through negotiations and the mediation process.

Sometimes, when parties talk directly to each other in a way that's organic and constructive, the mediator may be in the happy position of not being needed. At these points, the mediator may stay silent—and even push her chair back from the table—as a small sign that the parties are engaging well without her participation.

In what other ways will the mediator help move things forward between the parties?

Later on in the mediation, the mediator may help the parties decide which ideas make sense to include in a final agreement about how to move forward. For instance, maybe the two coworkers have had trouble agreeing on how often to meet so one can give the other progress reports or they need to address differing definitions of what's within the scope of one coworker's domain where he has autonomy to work freely without consulting the manager. In these moments, the mediator may use the skill of reframing, introduced in Chapter 3, to help parties stay focused on meeting their needs and interests. Mediators may use the skill of reframing to help move conversations forward, on both substantive and emotional levels. Mediators Ken Cloke and Joan Goldsmith offer a more nuanced and empathic definition of reframing, which they say "consists of using empathy to find a fresh word, phrase, or statement that includes the most important content or meaning of what was said, while avoiding mistaken impressions created by poor choice of words."[2] At a mediation table, Cloke and Goldsmith explain, this might take the form of reframing problems as questions or issues rather than statements of fact or opinion—or reframing an issue in a way that doesn't threaten a

2. Ken Cloke & Joan Goldsmith, Resolving Conflicts at Work 112 (2000).

person's self-esteem or dignity. And by setting this example, the mediator could be inviting the parties to take a similar approach.

Remember the earlier discussion of reframing from negative to positive back in Chapter 3? Mediator Margaret Shaw recounts a powerful example of this type of reframing in *Stories Mediators Tell.* In an employment discrimination case, the monetary gap between the two sides had narrowed dramatically to $30,000, with the plaintiff coming down to $175,000 and the defendant coming up to $145,000. The plaintiff, George, was upset about the last offer, noting that he had dropped his demand $200,000—from $375,000 to $175,000.

Earlier in the day, Margaret had had a conversation with George in the hallway in which she had asked about his family and interests outside work. In his spare time, George enjoyed spending time with his family and fixing up his house, he said, though he was still making payments on his mortgage of $140,000. Remembering this, Margaret turned to George and said, "You know George . . . if you accept the company's offer, you know what that will mean? That will mean that you can pay off your mortgage!"[3] George thought about it and accepted the offer.

Because she took the time to learn more about George and his life, Margaret was able to offer him another way to look at the proposal on the table. While most workplace mediations don't involve an exchange of money, reframing one party's idea or offer so that the other party can see the value in it, in language that speaks to them, is a strategy that applies to workplace cases as well.

3. Margaret Shaw, *Random Conversation, in* Stories Mediators Tell 165, 166 (Eric R. Galton & Lela P. Love eds., 2012).

19

Will the Mediator Set Ground Rules?

Just as mediators have different styles, they have different preferences about how to handle ground rules, or guidelines for behavior, during the process. Some mediators never use them; others always announce them at the start. For those who use ground rules, here are some common ones:

- Be respectful
- Speak one at a time
- Speak for yourself or from your own experience
- Assume good intentions

Many mediators fall somewhere between the yes and no camps, choosing to address behavior during their pre-mediation conversations by asking each party what kind of communication guidelines are likely to encourage that party's full participation in the mediation session. Depending on each party's response, the mediator will probably tell the parties she'll take their ideas into account and also share some of her own ideas or suggestions in the mediation.

Ground rules come with pros and cons. On the plus side, both parties may appreciate having clear expectations and guidelines for how the mediation will proceed. However, if the mediator sets out rules at the start, even if he invites the parties to add to the list, one or both parties could feel that the mediator has become the teacher, and anyone who misbehaves in his classroom is a "bad actor"—hardly a great beginning.

And what about enforcement? If the mediator sets the rules, won't he have to be the one to enforce them at all times? Will the parties start to think of him as policing their behavior? How will that affect the rapport between mediator and parties?

Still other challenges: The mediator might not want one party to interrupt another (or raise a voice or use rough language), but what if the parties are OK with it? Furthermore, when does the mediator know if a party has good or bad intent? Is this view of intent based on the mediator's own interpretation—or how the other party responds to a comment? Even a guideline as apparently benign as "be respectful" can be problematic, since respectful may look different to different people, especially coworkers from different cultures, people with different work experiences, and those with different areas of expertise. In short: In setting ground rules, the mediator will probably be making some guesses or assumptions about what will work best for the parties, and those may be wrong.

There are other ways to promote a respectful, learning environment for a productive exchange. A mediator might begin, for example, by acknowledging that both parties have been going through a challenging time and expressing appreciation for their willingness to give mediation a try. Then the mediator could simply listen and watch, and if she sees something that appears unhelpful, she could ask the parties how they'd like to handle it. This way parties can organically create their own ground rules, tailored to their own communication preferences and needs, when and if they wish. And it takes the guesswork out of things.

Take a look at this moment from the first mediation session with Jina and Shaheen, colleagues at the senior center.

HOW WOULD YOU LIKE TO HANDLE THIS?

(The mediation with senior center colleagues Jina and Shaheen, continued)

Jina and Shaheen are both enthusiastic and energetic talkers, and at one point in the mediation, after they have started addressing each other directly, each one interrupts the other at least twice.

The conversation starts up again, but the mediator wonders whether this stop-and-start action bothers Shaheen and Jina (as it does the mediator), so she halts the exchange. "I notice that you've both winced a couple of times in the last few minutes," she says, "and I'm wondering whether interruptions are getting in the way. Would it make sense to talk about how you'd like to handle interruptions in the future?"

To the mediator's surprise, both women seem taken aback.

"Not at all," Shaheen says. "I know that Jina, like me, comes from a large family, where we both sometimes had to shout to be heard. Being interrupted is no big deal."

Jina nods.

"OK, then," the mediator says. "Fair enough. Let's keep going."

Sometimes it can be hard for the mediator to know if her read of the room, or what Koreans call *nunchi*, is correct, so asking the parties is always a good option. The answer may be surprising.

20

Who Controls the Process—the Parties or Mediator?

Mediators manage the process, and parties control the content. This is how many mediators describe their role, in training and at the mediation table. For a mediator, process choices might include any of the following:

- Whether the mediation begins with a joint session
- Whether the mediation includes private caucuses as well as joint sessions—and if so, how the private sessions are introduced and handled
- How the mediation begins: What's topic #1? Which party talks first?
- Whether to set ground rules from the start, address them as needed during the mediation, or let the parties decide how to handle things such as interruptions or personal attacks ahead of time or when they occur

Some mediators may explicitly invite input from the parties about the process—in private pre-mediation conversations or throughout the process. Then, having heard what parties think, mediators will decide whether to incorporate their suggestions or wishes.

Whatever involvement parties have in establishing process, most mediators will want to have the final say.

WHOSE PROCESS?

Avery has been working with two colleagues at a tech firm, Becky, who is the COO, and Jamison, its director of administration. Jamison says he's fed up with what he sees as Becky's condescending attitude and micromanaging. Becky, who everyone at the company assumes will someday succeed her mentor as CEO, says that's nonsense. Jamison, she says, does good work but has resisted every single change she's suggested since she assumed her position several months ago.

After the mediation, Avery meets with Becky (and later Jamison) to debrief, just to check in and find out how she's finding the process. In their confidential conversation, Becky tells Avery that she should watch a favorite business TED Talk of hers and introduce its themes into the mediation as a way to show Jamison how and why he needs to get on board with Becky's ideas. The TED Talk, she says, is so important that she plans to ask everyone in the company to view and discuss it.

Avery, thinking that Becky is really looking for someone to promote her message, not a mediator, does a little reality testing. How does Becky think Jamison would react if Avery suddenly changed course and started discussing the TED Talk, abandoning the mediation plan that everyone had agreed to? How might that affect Jamison's perception of Avery as an unbiased mediator?

After more back and forth aimed at understanding Becky's interests, Avery tells Becky that she has every right to communicate her vision to her employees; doing so is just not Avery's job. When she tells Becky she is considering withdrawing from the case, Becky asks her to reconsider. Jamison may be challenging to work with, she says, but his experience is extensive, replacing him would be very difficult, and so she'd like to continue working in mediation together. She won't mention the TED Talk, she promises, and she will respect the mediation plan they all agreed to and will remember that Avery controls the mediation process. Avery agrees to continue but reminds Becky that if she senses a need to tweak the process, she might revisit this conversation.

21

If the People at the Table Have Different Communication Styles, How Will the Mediator Manage This?

A worker, trying to help move a project along after a complicated meeting, sends his colleague an email. The response stuns him. "When you sent that follow-up email," his coworker asks, "was it to be helpful—or because you thought I was incompetent?"

A boss, always detail-oriented and increasingly concerned about a looming deadline, leaves a long memo on his direct report's desk. "Did you send me that two-page, single-spaced set of instructions to be thorough?" the recipient asks. "Or don't you trust me to do my job?"

Different communication styles sometimes make disagreements even worse. So it makes sense that these tensions would show up in mediation.

One way for a mediator to get out in front of this often-challenging reality is to discuss with each party in pre-mediation conversations what she or he or they can do to help make the mediation time as productive and comfortable as possible. As always, open-ended questions help start the conversation. "How do you like to communicate? How about your boss (or colleague)?" These seemingly simple questions sometimes prompt people to describe bothersome behavior of others, especially connected to the mode of communication (phone, email, text, in-person) and frequency (too often, not often enough, never) during times of stress or conflict. Once people are working together in mediation, however, they have an opportunity to change that dynamic.

For example, let's revisit the mediation between pharmaceutical firm colleagues Grace and Valentina, whose contrasting communication styles have exacerbated their differences in opinion on how to collaborate effectively. Grace, who thinks on her feet and is able to offer arguments and counterarguments on the fly, enjoys an active exchange of ideas with colleagues. Her colleague Valentina, however, is more of an internal processor; typically she listens to ideas and questions, takes time to reflect, and may even revisit the conversation later in the day or the following day. Once their differences in processing and communicating have been identified and understood—not as lack of interest or antagonism, but simply a difference—Valentina and Grace can discuss how to adjust or experiment with new ways of communicating in the mediation and beyond. For example, they may decide to try out deferring to each person's communication preference, with Grace feeling free to share her ideas and concerns in the moment and Valentina feeling free to take her time in responding. If this goes smoothly in the mediation, they may decide to use this same approach in their day-to-day interactions, and perhaps be ready to discuss and make adjustments in a follow-up session with the mediator.

22

How Can the Mediator Work with Strong Emotions?

People sometimes ask, "Aren't some cases just too emotional for mediation?" Or "How do you separate the emotions so that you can get to the real problems in the conflict?" As many mediators know, working with emotions is a central component of this work. Sometimes, it's the heart of the conflict.

Mediators approach working with emotions in many ways, including acknowledging any emotions that parties share verbally or nonverbally, inviting parties to talk about how they feel about the conflict and how it has affected them, and labeling emotions or Core Concerns when they come up.

For some parties, the mediation process may be the first time they feel heard emotionally and substantively (as it was for Braden, the employee who felt bullied and unable to participate in mediation) about the conflict they have been living with for some time. Once parties feel that their emotions have been acknowledged and recognized, many of them feel more able to problem-solve and discuss substantive issues constructively. How can you know when someone has felt heard? Sometimes it's obvious: The mediator's summary of the emotional toll is greeted with a resounding "Yes!" or "Exactly." Sometimes it's more subtle: A party who has been repeating a complaint over and over can finally move on to another topic.

Process options may be useful, too. Perhaps after acknowledging one person's strong emotional reaction to what was just said by the other party, the mediator notices that the reacting party is still breathing heavily and avoiding eye contact. "Is this a good time for a short break?" the mediator might ask. Or she may simply announce it's time to switch to private sessions. Stopping the action can help break up a dynamic—and give everyone time to recover.

What if the mediation is between a supervisor and a subordinate? What else should the mediator keep in mind in working with strong emotions in a case? A study of 168 parties and their mediators, spearheaded by Meriem Kalter and colleagues at KU Leuven in Belgium, provides a helpful data point. The study examined the accuracy with which mediators could assess their parties' positive and negative emotions in workplace mediations between supervisors and subordinates. In their analysis comparing the self-reported responses of parties to that of their mediators, the researchers found that mediators more accurately perceived the emotions of the supervisor-parties.

Why the discrepancy? The authors note that one possibility could be the caution or social constraint shown by subordinate parties given their lower power status. While acknowledging possible shortcomings to the study—that parties' responses may have been influenced by a desire to present themselves in a positive light or by recall bias, given the time lag between the mediation and when parties were asked to reflect on their experience—the authors urge mediators to pay particular attention to the emotions of subordinate parties. More specifically, they suggest that mediators check their perception of a party's emotions to confirm their perception is correct. For example, they suggest directly asking a party how they are feeling. A mediator might say, "You seem like you're still angry about the conflict. Is that right?" This form of paraphrasing, the final step in a "looping" paraphrase to confirm understanding, is helpful at many stages, but it's a key way to explore and accurately understand the strong emotions of a party, subordinate or supervisor.

23

How Can the Mediator Address a Power Imbalance?

In many cases, the parties in a workplace mediation are in a reporting relationship, directly or indirectly. On the surface, this might seem especially challenging, but many experienced mediators see a power imbalance as an opportunity to create an environment that enables equal participation.

Remember Becky, the COO, and Jamison, the director of administration? Knowing that Becky's mentor founded the company and that Becky is probably going to be CEO soon, Jamison might easily feel that the cards are stacked against him. What could the mediator Avery do to enable Jamison to participate fully? Because the difference in formal authority is obvious to everyone—after all, if she wanted to, Becky could fire Jamison—as she starts working with these two, Avery could clearly communicate how she envisions the mediation process—and ask Jamison and Becky how she can help them throughout. Some possible questions aimed at getting to this:

- What can Avery do in the mediation to support Jamison's full participation in the process? If Jamison says Becky often interrupts him, for example, what, if anything, would Jamison like Avery to do?

- Would Becky and Jamison like to have discussion questions and/or agenda items in advance of the mediation session, so that each one has time to reflect on them and arrive prepared to discuss them?
- If Jamison has expressed concern about being overshadowed or outdone, would he feel more comfortable if Avery provided more structure—in other words, if Avery facilitated more actively—at least at the start of the mediation?
- What other information—about the role of the mediator, about the mediation process, or anything else—would be helpful?

Given the research described in Chapter 12 about subordinates feeling less satisfied with mediation when they felt uncertain about it, these sorts of questions could help ease concern and demystify the process. Some could be addressed to both Becky and Jamison, but some, such as the one about providing more structure, might best be put only to the person with less power (in this case, Jamison). For example, Avery may want to ask Jamison how he would like the mediation to start—Would he like to speak first? After Becky?—as a way to acknowledge the power imbalance and invite Jamison to jump in.

Avery might also check in with Becky to find out how she's doing with all of this. Does she think that this attention to Jamison makes sense, or does she feel that it favors Jamison? If she feels that she is ceding some of the authority that typically attaches to all her interactions as a senior leader in the workplace, Becky might be uncomfortable, so the mediator should explore how best to structure the process so that Becky feels her status is respected (though perhaps in a different way from what she is used to).

The mediator may also want to consider how a power imbalance might affect how parties discuss the commitments they make in mediation. In their research of workplace mediations between supervisors and subordinates, University of Leuven researcher Kalter and her colleagues Katalien Bollen and Martin Euwema found that these parties may have different perceptions of agreement compliance, suggesting that mediators should help parties carefully think through compliance with any terms they agree to. Mindful of the hesitation a subordinate might feel about raising the question of noncompliance with a supervisor, the authors suggest that the mediator herself might raise the topic—and let the parties decide how they want to deal with it.

The bottom line: Power imbalances present unique challenges in mediation. The right approach may not be clear at the start, so a bit of experimentation and a lot of discussion might be needed.

Incorporating lessons from dialogue

Because workplace mediations often focus on resetting or resuming dialogue between coworkers, the field of dialogue can provide helpful ideas, especially in cases where one party has more power than another. In many instances, this power imbalance, and the associated dynamics, is a reason the parties are in mediation. With the aim of leveling the power imbalance in mediation, mediators may want to include some of these specific dialogic practices:

- **Connecting question.** Essential Partners, which helps civic groups, faith communities, workplaces, and other organizations foster understanding and trust through dialogue, describes a connecting question as an "opportunity to share something new, break a stereotype, humanize one another, and serve as the first step toward a deeper relationship." Opening with a connecting question such as "What drew you to your work?" can serve to welcome both parties into the mediation space and encourage them to get to know each other in a new way. (More information on sample connecting questions that might be applicable or adapted for workplace mediations can be found in the Bibliography.)
- **Time-limited responses.** Setting limits on responses to certain questions ("How about each of you try to answer this in about two minutes?") can promote equal airtime.
- **Time for reflection.** Adding time for people to reflect on their own or another's responses to questions, either beforehand or in the mediation itself, can help both parties feel better prepared to participate.
- **A dialogic environment.** Urging parties to think of the conversation as an opportunity to share and learn, not to persuade, can promote what's called a dialogic (not adversarial) environment.

Remember Jina and her supervisor Shaheen at the local senior center? Here's how things might have played out after they signed the Agreement to Mediate.

WHAT BRINGS YOU JOY?

Hoping to encourage Jina and Shaheen to think about what connects (not divides) them, at the start of the mediation the mediator poses one question to both parties at the table: "What brings you joy in your work?"

After taking some time to think, Jina says that she lost her mom suddenly, and working with the seniors at the center now brings her some peace, comfort, and joy, especially when she misses her mother. Shaheen then says that she wishes a center, like the one where they now work, had been available for her dad when he arrived from India in his later years. He often felt isolated, she says, and had little or no chance to connect with others.

In beginning a tough conversation this way, the mediator gives Jina and Shaheen a chance to see each other in a different way and—ideally—sense a connection in their love for their parents and wish to help seniors in their community.

24

What About Bias?

In recent years, an increasing number of workplace mediations have centered on perceptions of bias, including cases in which both parties believe they have been treated differently based on one or more of their known identities. Although issues of bias sometimes present as the main issue in the mediation (i.e., the mediation was prompted by an allegation of bias or discrimination), bias can surface in other ways that mediators should be aware of.

Raising awareness about cognitive and implicit biases

In *Stories Mediators Tell,* mediator Eric Galton recounts an exchange in a race discrimination mediation in which he regretted his quick read of a party. The plaintiff's lawyer had asked Eric to speak with his client James, to help the client understand that the offer on the table was one that warranted serious consideration. After James asks Eric to give him one good new reason he should accept the offer, Eric explains his next move: "I told James that I didn't know if he'd been paying attention to the political realities in the great state of Texas these past fifteen years, but in case he'd been sleeping, I felt that I should point out that we'd been living under Republican rule. And that meant that all the appellate judges were Republican, and they'd never met an insurance company or big business institution they didn't like. I told James that a jury might give him a lot of money, but three years later those Republican appellate judges would devour him and spit him out and he would walk away with nothing."[1]

Eric thought this was a compelling reason to accept the settlement offer from the defendant. The problem with this one good reason? James was vice chair of the county's Republican party, so Eric's comment offended him. Deeply.

Whatever style or process they prefer, mediators agree that the mediator's neutrality is a crucial part of the process. While a mediator's internal thoughts and feelings might lean one way—in favor or against a party—the mediator is charged with behaving in an impartial manner toward the parties and with respect to the outcome. Because if a mediator is perceived as stereotyping or exhibiting a bias of some kind, as Eric was, this can easily erode or break any trust with a party that the mediator has worked hard to build.

What, exactly, is bias? And what's the definition of "neutral"? Mediators disagree on what neutrality looks like, and some even say it's a myth because every mediator is human, and all humans react to what they see and hear. The article title "Implicit Bias and the Illusion of Mediator Neutrality," by UC San Francisco emerita law professor Carol Izumi, succinctly captures this dilemma for mediators. Social science research on implicit bias, notably by psychologists Mahzarin Banaji of Harvard University and Anthony Greenwald of the University of Washington, has now entered the mainstream consciousness, confirming that we all carry implicit biases—unconscious stereotypes and associations that we've acquired from years of exposure to attitudes about race, age, gender, religion, class, sexual orientation, ability, nationality, and other attributes. Yet mediators, like judges, are still expected to act impartially toward the parties at their table.

Given these realities, mediators should take steps to raise their awareness about unconscious or implicit bias that could influence their behavior toward the parties. In their article, "Follow the Science: Proven Strategies for Reducing Unconscious Bias," mediators David Hoffman

---

1. Eric Galton, *A Blunder, in* Stories Mediators Tell 277, 280 (Eric R. Galton & Lela P. Love eds., 2012).

and Helen Winter describe the social science research supporting several bias-reduction strategies. Three of them—increasing self-awareness, a motivation to counteract implicit bias, and perspective-taking (the ability to understand and consider another person's thoughts, feelings, and beliefs)—are accessible strategies that mediators can employ to assist in their efforts to be impartial as they work with mediation parties. With this in mind, to raise their self-awareness, many mediators engage in some type of reflection at the outset of a new mediation, aiming to identify positive or negative connections or associations they may have about the people or facts of a case.

What about cognitive biases? While implicit bias has to do with unconscious mental associations or stereotypes, cognitive biases are a type of unconscious bias that relate to faulty reasoning or systematic errors in thinking. So mediators should also consider how cognitive biases might affect their impartiality. Here is a brief overview of a few cognitive biases especially relevant to mediation:

Confirmation bias is a type of cognitive bias that involves favoring new information that confirms your previously existing beliefs. For example, if the mediator practiced employment discrimination law as a plaintiff's attorney for many years, based on that experience she may see a new discrimination case in a way that matches many of her past cases. In her book *Thinking 101*, Yale psychology professor Woo-Kyoung Ahn suggests that people ask themselves a question framed in two opposite ways to try to counteract the earlier confirmation bias. So in the prior example, the lawyer-turned-mediator might be curious to see and learn how the current mediation differs from prior mediations and ask herself, "How is the case similar to some of my past discrimination cases?" as well as "How is this case different?" Might there be an important nuance that puts the underlying conflict or the parties in a different light? Engaging in this sort of examination might lead the mediator to come to a different understanding or conclusion. Psychological studies confirm the value of this approach: in *Psychology for Lawyers*, Robbennolt and Sternlight note that the "consider the opposite" strategy has been found to be more effective in decreasing reliance on preconceptions than a good faith effort to do so.

Affinity bias is our unconscious preference for people who are similar to us or whom we know and like. Many of us are familiar with this concept in the workplace, especially in hiring or promotion decisions, which can lead to managers hiring people who look and act like themselves. Affinity can extend to family ties, responsibilities, and even humor, so a mediator should be wary of feeling positive bias toward someone with whom she shares an experience, connection, or even just a sense of what's funny. A mediator with two young daughters, for example, might feel an immediate affinity with a woman whose children are about the same age. These kinds of connections can surface during pre-mediation discussions or even during small talk in a joint session. Remember the conflict between Jina and Shaheen at the senior center? What if, in the pre-mediation conversation, Jina tells the mediator that she thinks some of her dislike of Shaheen is related to her experiences in her own family, where Jina, the youngest of three sisters, often felt that she was being bossed around by her siblings? If the mediator also has two strong-minded older sisters, she might have to stop and catch herself from nodding with understanding—and focus on remaining impartial.

Although much of the advice on counteracting affinity bias comes from the realm of human resources and focuses on hiring and promotion, mediators can apply similar strategies, aiming to find a connection with a party, for example, after sensing a tie with the other. More broadly, as recommended by *Harvard Business Review* contributor Ruchika T. Malhotra in "How to Reduce Personal Bias When Hiring," a mediator could embark on a perspective-taking strategy, spending time reading and learning about the experiences of other social groups. Other studies, included in the Hoffman and Winter article mentioned earlier, recommend working to expand personal and professional networks to include people from different backgrounds and experiences as a longer-term strategy to counteract biases.

The ***halo effect*** happens when a positive single trait or quality of someone influences your overall perception of them. Psychologist Daniel Kahneman describes it as the "tendency to like (or dislike) everything about a person—including things you have not observed" and further explains that the sequence in which we observe a person's characteristics matters: The halo effect "increases the weight of first impressions, sometimes to the point that subsequent information is mostly wasted."[2] The

2. Daniel Kahneman, Thinking, Fast and Slow 82–83 (2011).

reverse, the *horn effect*, is when a negative trait or quality of someone leads you to assume the worst about them. The halo effect might come into play in a workplace mediation over multiple sessions, especially when one party seems to be more engaged, constructive, responsive, or attentive.

The horn effect could easily come into play as well. Let's revisit the mediation between COO Becky and Jamison, the company's director of administration.

TRYING TO GET A WORD IN EDGEWISE

In a pre-mediation conversation with mediator Avery, Becky talks animatedly about her background, how she learned about the business from her mentor and how frustrated she has felt with what she sees as Jamison's undermining of her authority. Every time Avery senses a slight pause in which she can pose a question to Becky or share information about the mediation process, Becky launches into another story about the workplace, and Avery can feel her own frustration beginning to build.

What should she do? In "The Halo Effect: What It Is and How to Beat It," psychologist Eva Krockow recommends slowing down and working to control subjective feelings as strategies to reduce the influence of cognitive biases like the halo (or horn) effect. Applying these steps to the mediation scenario, Avery could first notice the negative impression she is starting to form about Becky, remind herself to avoid making character judgments based on this first interaction, and acknowledge that with time and more interactions, she will gain a fuller understanding or impression of Becky. She could also consider alternate reasons for Becky's behavior. For example, perhaps Becky is nervous and feels uncomfortable being asked to participate in mediation, and that's driving her nonstop talk.

If these biases operate at an unconscious level, what can or should a mediator do about them? The first critical step for a mediator interested in combatting cognitive and implicit biases is to take steps to make the unconscious conscious. Including a self-reflective step is one way to do so. Given the challenge of surfacing the unconscious, a mediator may opt to engage in conversation with peers (co-mediators or fellow mediators) on this topic, much as psychologists engage in peer supervision. In peer supervision, clinicians bring specific consultation questions to the group and the group peer members, from a nonjudgmental place, provide support to the therapist with the goal of improving patient care. Similarly, while a mediator may not be able to reliably identify an unconscious bias that may be coming up for her related to a given mediation, a peer, in asking thoughtful questions ("What might be coming up for you as you learned more about this party?") and sharing ideas, as a clinician would, might be able to help the mediator raise her own self-awareness. In addition to helping a mediator identify a cognitive bias, either of these steps may also provide another data point for the mediator as she understands the dynamics of the case. For example, if she is noticing a negative or mixed reaction to a party's behavior, is that how they are received by others? How might this be impacting the conflict at hand?

Another way to encapsulate this advice is to take a step back and try to see the parties more three-dimensionally. This approach, advocated by mediator David Hoffman, encourages us to look and think beyond our initial impressions (or even unconscious associations) to appreciate the complexity within each of us.

Once she becomes aware of a bias (in favor or against a party), what can a mediator do to help manage her reactions? Mindfulness might help. Mediator and Northwestern University law professor Len Riskin has been a longtime proponent of the use of mindfulness in dispute resolution. In an interview, he recounted realizing he had developed an "aversion" to one party in a mediation and how mindfulness helped him rebalance his feelings: "Once I started to notice the aversion," he said "I was able to let it go instead of getting caught up in how much I disliked the party. I was able to notice that I was having that reaction and just let it be there. I didn't let my reaction to the man control what I was feeling."[3]

In thinking about implicit and cognitive biases, parties can help here, too: As noted before, many mediators ask parties at the start to speak up

3. Linda Lazarus, "A Conversation with Professor Leonard Riskin about Mindfulness, Dispute Resolution, and Mindfulness Resources for Mediators," www.mediate.com (Feb. 22, 2005), https://mediate.com/a-conversation-with-professor-leonard-riskin-about-mindfulness-dispute-resolution-and-mindfulness-resources-for-mediators/.

if they think the mediator is saying or doing something that they think shows favoritism or bias. The *perception* of bias is powerful; even if the mediator doesn't think she's favoring someone, she needs to be aware that a party may see bias in her behavior. If a party expresses concern and remains concerned, he or she or the neutral might need to end the mediation, perhaps with the hope of finding another mediator.

As a closing thought, mediators might want to keep Eric Galton's reflections in mind. After reflecting on his big blunder about Texas Republicans, Eric devised a new mantra for himself, one of humility, that he tries to recall before every mediation. "I remind myself that I know absolutely nothing about any of the people I am about to meet," he says, "and that my mission is to get to know each of them and what is important to each of them."[4]

Addressing bias in the mediation

Parties sometimes say or do something in mediation that the mediator interprets as biased against the other party or mediator. What should the mediator do? Imagine the following: You are a 35-year-old female mediator working on a sexual harassment case. Late in the afternoon of the one-day mediation, after caucusing first with a manager and then with a female employee who has accused him of making inappropriate remarks, you return to caucus with the manager to discuss the latest proposal. After you comment on the progress that's been made thus far, the manager turns to you, looking a bit doubtful, and says, "Were you a cheerleader in high school?"

When presented with this scenario in trainings and asked how they would respond, people have offered wildly different answers. Some said they would be deeply offended—and would probably have to work hard to restrain themselves from saying so. The boss's comment, they said, is obviously intended to belittle the mediator's experience and status. (A sample mediator response from this camp might be, "No. Were *you*???") But others didn't take offense. One male mediator who went to an all-boys school with only male cheerleaders, had no problem with the

4. Galton, *supra* note 1, at 282.

remark. Another mediator, a retired judge, said she had been a cheerleader. In her day, being on the cheerleading squad was considered a huge accomplishment, so why would she mind?

As these comments show, each mediator will probably interpret (and respond to) any given remark differently, based mostly on their own unique history, experiences, and mental shortcuts. So in these instances, a mediator might approach making a response just as she would other issues in mediation: by considering both process and substance.

On the substance, a mediator may ask herself:

- What can I learn from the party's comment or question?
- Is the party giving voice to an unmet need or interest?

In terms of process, the mediator might ask herself:

- What time would be best to broach the topic (i.e., now or later in the process)?
- What place (joint session versus caucus) would be better for exploring the comment?

Some mediators might feel no need to respond directly—they might believe that their role is solely or primarily to assist the parties in trying to reach a resolution, and any personal reaction (if they have one) is secondary. Others may feel a need to respond to the comment based on their personal beliefs or values. In some instances, a mediator's decision may also be influenced by the context or referral of the case—a government mediator, for instance, might feel more constrained in expressing displeasure than a private mediator, while a social justice mediator for a nonprofit advocacy group might feel compelled to let the speaker know that the comment could be interpreted as a stereotype.

HERE WE GO AGAIN

In a workplace case between two colleagues, an older White woman, Linda, and a younger Latina manager named Vanessa, Linda says in joint session that Vanessa is "just so inexperienced and unprofessional." The mediator knows from a pre-mediation call with the younger manager that Vanessa feels that Linda has repeatedly belittled her training and work experience, a slight she has encountered before as an up-and-coming Latina in the field, and that this has fueled much of the conflict.

Vanessa, sitting across from Linda, says nothing after the comment but sighs, crosses her arms, and angles her body away from the table.

What should the mediator do?

When mediators and trainees discuss this scenario, as with the cheerleader comment, ideas about how to respond are based on how each mediator interprets the comment, his or her mediation style, and sometimes how they see their role as mediator. For example: If in doubt as to what Linda intended to accomplish with the comment, the mediator could fall back on her initial mediation training and seek to clarify by asking Linda, "Could you say more about that?" Or the mediator could move to check in with the manager, Vanessa, either in joint or private session. Alternatively, some mediators and trainees suggest, having noticed Vanessa's reaction, the mediator could comment on Vanessa's body language and ask her if she wants to respond to Linda.

Whatever the mediator chooses to do next, inquiring about the intent of Linda's comment could be helpful, as Linda could be unaware of how her words land—and how Vanessa might see them as hurtful stereotyping. In an ideal world, this might be an opportunity for both parties to share how their experiences—personal and professional—influence how they show up at work, how they interact with each other, and what they hope for. And this could help them talk about how they can move forward together as colleagues.

Managing issues related to implicit or cognitive biases is challenging. As mediators navigate this terrain, the following might be helpful considerations:

1. *Be purposeful*
   - Know your choices will have an impact.
   - Consider process options (joint and private sessions).
2. *Remember: interpretations vary*
   - Yours is not necessarily theirs.
   - Curiosity is a helpful resource.
3. *Reflect on your personal style and approach*
   - How do you see your role?
   - How do your personal values affect your role as mediator?
   - If you are a member of a mediation panel or volunteer mediator with a community mediation program, what are the values of your organization—and how might they affect how you approach your mediations?

Wrapping Up

25

How Long Do These Mediations Usually Last?

Most workplace cases, particularly those involving a continuing relationship, take more than one mediation session. Parties tend to be just as aware of the clock as the mediator is, so as time is running out in the first session, most mediators try to summarize where things stand at that moment and discuss next steps. If everyone is on board, the mediator may propose a follow-up session and let the parties know she's available for one-on-one debriefings or prep conversations with each side before that next session takes place.

In the follow-up debrief or prep conversation, the mediator may want to ask the following questions (or some variation):

- How do you think things went in the first session?
- What was helpful—and should we continue doing it?
- What should we consider changing?
- Any other thoughts about the first session?
- How do you feel about the joint session time in the first meeting?
- What, if anything, would you like to approach differently in terms of process?
- What topics would you like to explore in the next session?

With open-ended inquiries such as these, the mediator can gain valuable information about how best to meet the needs of each party and how to structure and facilitate the next session.

26

If the Parties Reach an Agreement, Who Will Put It into Writing?

The parties are responsible for the substance of any mediated agreement. This reality means that in mediation, the parties have the power to decide for themselves what is best, and the mediator oversees the process. If the parties reach an agreement, the mediator can and often does serve in a facilitative role as scribe, memorializing the parties' ideas. The mediator may also help the parties decide on specifics to make their agreement durable and actionable, asking clarifying questions such as:

- What is the deadline for each action item?
- Who will be responsible for initiating each action item?
- How will the parties handle future conflicts or difficulties if they arise?

At this stage, hoping to help ensure that the agreement covers all the items that each party considers important, the mediator may also pose more substantive questions to one or both parties. Let's revisit the mediation between Valentina and Grace, colleagues at the pharmaceutical firm. In a later mediation session, the parties ask the mediator's help to put their agreements into an email they can keep for future reference. As the parties figure out wording for a bullet-point list of terms regarding how they will approach differences of opinion in the future, the mediator Jamal, as scribe, might say to Valentina, who has been silent on this point, "Valentina, I know you said earlier that you feel most comfortable having some notice before engaging in a substantive conversation that might take you off guard. Given that, do you have a suggestion for how Grace should approach you if she wants to discuss a change in how you're working together?"

With this type of follow-up question, which Avery used with Becky, the soon-to-be CEO, the mediator is engaging in "reality testing," doublechecking to see whether an idea really meets a party's needs or interests. The goal of all this is simple: creating an agreement that is clear, has no ambiguities, and addresses everything that's important to both parties.

Two quick comments on writing up agreements:

- Mediators who are not lawyers should note that to avoid the unauthorized practice of law, they should take care to put into writing only the terms specified by the parties. In their article, "A Mediator's Obligation to Memorialize the Agreement," Hamline Law professor Sharon Press and Paul Laurie, a lawyer with Schiff Hardin, call this "memorializing." Memorializing an agreement is fine; drafting one, using language provided by the nonlawyer mediator, is not.
- For lawyer-mediators, the guidance is clear on the importance of the lawyer-mediator clarifying her role as neutral and not advocate, especially in the later stages of mediation, such as in the agreement-writing phase. On this point, Formal Opinion 518 of the American Bar Association explains that the lawyer-mediator should not state that she is "acting to achieve a party's best interest or that a proposed settlement is in a party's best interest"—language that a party could interpret as advice from a lawyer. If the parties want the agreement to be legally enforceable and neither has a lawyer, they should each consult lawyers to advise them and draft the agreement.

27

What About Enforcement?

As I mentioned near the start of this book, unlike mediations involving business deals, divorce, or other matters, many workplace mediations do not result in formal, signed agreements that include financial terms or compensation. Because these mediations usually focus on helping coworkers understand their workplace dynamic, repair past injuries, and move forward productively, the result of many workplace mediations is a repaired relationship, improved and deeper understanding of each other, or shared agreements for interacting and communicating in the future.

Sometimes the parties are content with verbal agreements for these more informal outcomes, while other times these commitments are memorialized in some way, perhaps in an email written by the mediator. If parties have agreed to important action steps in mediation, they may want to write up their agreement in a more formal way, such as in a memorandum of understanding that might even have a term related to the parties' intent for the agreement to be legally binding. But many times, the agreement is informal and oral, instead of written.

People tend to value things they have crafted themselves, so most mediation participants who have spelled out their own agreements tend to honor them. What if someone doesn't? Some agreements mention what should happen if one party violates the agreement, which the parties may only decide upon once they've determined the terms of their agreement. Other agreements might note (or the mediator and parties might remind each other in the mediation) that both parties can consult resources in their own organization, such as an HR officer or ombuds, for guidance if they can do so without breaking the agreed-upon confidentiality of the mediation process. Because the mediator's role does not include an enforcement ability, the parties are ultimately on their own to carry out their commitments. The good news here is that parties usually comply with mediated resolutions because any agreements have been crafted by them to meet their own interests.

At this stage, a related question may come up: Who else can know about the mediated agreement, if anyone, other than the parties? Should the referring manager or HR director learn about the commitments or action steps the parties have set out? If the parties agree on specific steps, such as training for a department or assignments for one party, other people may need to have awareness of the agreement or even input (which would mean that the agreement would also probably be written). If the parties agree that an internal complaint will be dropped, others will need to be informed to make that happen.

If the parties do write up their agreement as a formal, signed memorandum of understanding, they should know that a signed mediated agreement—even one discussing relationships and behavior—might be considered a legally enforceable contract. Practically speaking, because most workplace mediation agreements focus on specific relational behaviors (such as "Linda agrees to ask Vanessa about new work projects before committing resources to them"), the likelihood that one party will take the other to court alleging breach of contract seems quite small. (If this section has piqued your interest, see "Enforceability of Agreements" in David Hoffman's book, *Mediation: A Practice Guide for Mediators, Lawyers, and Other Professionals*, for a more in-depth analysis.)

28

What Happens If a Mediation Is Not Fully Successful?

What if the mediation addresses some—but not all—of the sources of tension between two colleagues? What if they come to some agreement about how to move forward, but one person is still uncomfortable or upset with the other?

Not all mediations will address every aspect of the conflict between parties. Mediators have been debating the definition of the word "success" for decades, and the word still means different things to different people, including both parties and neutrals (as the story of mediator Olivia and Braden, who felt too vulnerable to mediate, might illustrate). For many mediators and some parties, success in mediation might simply be learning something new or coming to a deeper understanding—about the other party, themselves, or how to move forward together.

That being said, if the mediation ends without any deeper understanding between the parties or agreement about future behavior and cooperation, one or both parties and the mediator might feel unsatisfied. Not every mediation concludes with a Hollywood ending, and disappointing conclusions can be caused by many factors. Maybe one party (or both parties) just wasn't ready. Maybe someone felt overwhelmed or unable to contribute, and the mediator's efforts to help him or her weren't enough to allow full participation. Sometimes a disciplinary measure just won't wait.

Whenever a party or mediator chooses to end a mediation because of one of these realities, the mediator should acknowledge the effort involved in trying, remind everyone about the confidentiality of the process, and confirm next steps (which could simply be telling the employer contact that mediation has concluded). Endings, especially unsatisfying ones, are never easy, but they can lead to meaningful post-mediation steps, for both mediator and parties.

29

What Post-Mediation Steps Should a Mediator Take?

The parties might consider the mediation over at the conclusion of the last session, but a mediator who wants to be thorough, serve the parties well, and learn from her experience will do several things before moving on.

With parties. During the final mediation session, most mediators will verbally summarize any agreements or action steps and seek further input from the parties:

- Would they like the mediator to prepare a written summary and email it to them?
- What, if anything, are the parties comfortable having the mediator share with the employer contact?
- How about scheduling a check-in time in a few weeks (or months), just to see how things are going?
- If the parties need help down the road, who will they reach out to? The mediator? The employer contact? A manager or someone in HR?

With the employer contact. As I mentioned before, what will—and will not—be shared with the employer contact is a topic that should be addressed at the very beginning of the process, before the mediator even reaches out to the parties for pre-mediation conversations. At a minimum, most employer contacts want to be informed about the status of the mediation—How many meetings have been held? How many more are expected?—so the mediator will let the employer contact know when mediation work has concluded. At this time, the mediator may also need to prepare and send invoices.

A wrap-up conversation with the employer contact can be another helpful step for closure. Perhaps the contact has a question about how best to note that the employees participated in mediation. (For instance, many HR professionals keep mediation files, electronic or physical, separate from the employee's personnel file.) Or the contact may have questions about next steps for the parties. Although sometimes parties choose to share some or all of their agreement with the employer contact, if they have not, the HR director who hired the mediator might be eager to know how to support the two employees going forward, without knowing any of the details from the mediation discussions. In such cases, unless the parties have specifically agreed to allow disclosure about content, the mediator can respect the confidentiality of the process by suggesting that the employer contact pose that same question to the parties. "How can I help?" is almost always a welcome question.

With a co-mediator. Most mediators work solo, but some may co-mediate when one practitioner is mentoring another, when a community mediation center is involved, or in cases where the employer contact believes that two individuals from different backgrounds would be helpful. Any two people will have two perspectives on one mediation and its parties, so taking care to provide space for mediators to debrief in private and at length can be very valuable, as co-mediators can discuss their different experiences and review difficult moments.

Debriefing the experience—on your own or with others. If a mediator works solo, she might want to take a few moments after the last session to reflect on the mediation and identify learnings to take forward, alone or with colleagues—always being careful to honor confidentiality.

Talking with the parties individually after the mediation has had time to settle can also be instructive. Remember mediator Zaineb's post-mediation debrief with Becca, who said she was disappointed she hadn't gotten more personal coaching? Learning about such things after a mediation has ended can help the mediator avoid a similar misunderstanding (or misperception) in the future.

If you're in a coaching role, the same thinking applies. Remember Morgan and Alex? Since their manager's skillful coaching and discussions about interests, perceptions, relationships, and advocacy, Morgan and Alex have been working well, communicating more regularly and enjoying a more relaxed dynamic as they rebuild trust. Their manager wants to support this new rapport. What can she do? Either separately or together, she can invite Alex and Morgan to talk about how things are going. What is working well in their working relationship? What concerns might be helpful to address now, before too much time passes and the concerns grow? In this way, the manager-coach can signal that new working relationship dynamics take time and attention—and she's eager to help.

For practitioners who work alone, mediation can be a solitary business, but finding a colleague to talk with about challenging moments (always changing details and avoiding information that would violate confidentiality) can go a long way toward easing the sense of isolation. Some self-reflective debrief questions may include:

- What one approach to the mediation (or to a difficult moment) worked well and would be helpful to remember for next time?
- What was a challenging mediation moment that could be handled differently in the future? What might that look like?
- Looking back on this mediation, what might be a good change to make in preparing for your next case?

CONCLUSION

Congratulations on making it to the end of the book. Whether you've read it from start to finish or referred to it for help with a particular part of the mediation process, I hope you've found it useful. Or maybe a conversation starter—with fellow colleagues in mediation, HR, or employment law. I said at the start that I wanted to offer information and encouragement, but by discussing each stage of this particular kind of work, I also hope I've helped demystify the process of workplace mediation and perhaps encouraged people to consider giving it a try. And as you do, I welcome hearing your ideas, suggestions, and thoughts about the book.

***

In wrapping up, I'd like to take a step back and widen the lens. At its best, workplace mediation can be life-changing, in small, if not large, ways. Two colleagues can go from the brink of a lawsuit to genuine friendship, camaraderie, and concern for each other. I've seen that happen—and, of course, cases in which the final result falls short of it. Not all workplace conflict mediations will be transformative (in the wide, non-mediation meaning of the word), but the power of engaging in the process and working with a mediator can fundamentally change how people experience their work, how they see themselves, and how they carry themselves in their workplace and at home.

A parting thought to those who might be reading this in a moment of discouragement. Maybe you feel you handled a mediation poorly, or you're discouraged because a party left a session upset or even ended the process early. In spite of our best intentions and our hard-earned skills, all of us who do this work and set high standards for ourselves have moments when we feel we've let the parties—or ourselves—down. The truth is, navigating workplace conflict can be difficult. Whether you're in the thick of it yourself, coaching a colleague, or working with parties as a mediator, workplace conflict can leave you feeling uncomfortable, uncertain, and unhappy. But remember: Even without a clear resolution or "win," the act of thoughtfully engaging in a process, in direct dialogue or mediation, and being present to hear someone's needs, concerns, and hopes can have a positive impact.

A quote often attributed to Maya Angelou is one I like to remember when reflecting on this work. "I've learned that people will forget what you said and people will forget what you did, but people will never forget how you made them feel." While we may experience uncertainty at any given moment, as mediators we strive to be and stay grounded and in the moment. In our increasingly busy, impersonal, tech-filled world, this can be our biggest contribution. We can help people feel more centered, valued, or appreciated. And that may be the best start to improving conflict at work—and beyond.

Appendix A

Prep Checklist for Your Workplace Conflict

I. Interests and Priorities

What interests do you hope to satisfy in the conversation? __________ __________ __________	What interests might the other person hope to satisfy in the conversation? __________ __________ __________
How would you prioritize your goals? Rank them in order of priority. __________ __________ __________	What might be their priorities for the conversation? __________ __________ __________

II. Perceptions of Background Events

Your Perception: How would you describe the background events giving rise to the current situation? __________ __________ __________	*Their Perception*: How might the other person describe the background events giving rise to the current situation? __________ __________ __________
What facts or information (relevant to or outside of this situation) would support or confirm your perspective on background events? __________ __________ __________	What facts or information (relevant to or outside of this situation) would support or confirm their perspective on background events? __________ __________ __________

III. Relationship Audit

What is the relationship like now? __________ __________ __________	What are general strategies to improve it? __________ __________ __________
Why might it be that way? __________ __________ __________	Specific action items? __________ __________ __________

IV. Managing the Conversation

Advocacy	*Inquiry*
Given your perception of background events and your interests, how will you begin the conversation? What will you say? __________ __________ __________	What will you ask to learn more about their perception of background events and their interests in the conversation? __________ __________ __________
How will you convey what is most important to you? __________ __________ __________	How will you learn what is most important to them? What will you ask? __________ __________ __________
Knowing what you know about the other person, what would be the most effective way to frame your message to this person? __________ __________ __________	What information would you like to learn from the other person (which might confirm or challenge your perception of background events and of them)? __________ __________ __________

Appendix B

Sample Workplace Agreement to Mediate

This sample Agreement to Mediate was created by Boston Law Collaborative, LLC. Note that there is some language in this Agreement that would be relevant only if the mediator is an attorney, as is the case for mediators at Boston Law Collaborative. As with other aspects of mediation, mediators will want to tailor their Agreement to Mediate to suit their own and their clients' needs. While some mediators may use a shorter Agreement in their practice, this sample is provided in the hopes that it will serve as a comprehensive example of what might be included, with language that mediators might find helpful in crafting their own Agreements.

AGREEMENT TO MEDIATE

The undersigned parties (collectively, the "Parties") have agreed to participate in a voluntary, nonbinding mediation conducted by ____________ (the "Mediator"). The Parties and the Mediator agree as follows:

1. **The Mediation Process**
   The purpose of the mediation process is to assist the Parties in reaching agreement on ways to improve communication and work together going forward.

a. Role of the Mediator. The Mediator's role is to serve as an impartial facilitator of the discussions. The Mediator has no power to order or dictate any terms of any agreement—all such power belongs to the Parties.
b. Voluntary process. Either Party may terminate the mediation for any reason by written notification to the Mediator and to the other Party. The Mediator may terminate his/her participation in the mediation if (1) the EMPLOYER fails to pay for the Mediator's services, (2) continuation of the mediation would involve a violation of applicable ethical rules, or (3) other reasonable cause; in the event of such termination, the Mediator shall maintain the confidentiality of all information to which the obligation of confidentiality applies under this Agreement.
c. Respectful communications. The Parties agree that respectful communications are essential to the mediation process and that they shall endeavor to communicate with each other in that manner.

2. **Legal Representation**

The Parties understand that the Mediator is not undertaking to provide legal advice or representation on behalf of any Party in connection with the mediation and [if the mediator is also an attorney] shall not represent either Party as an attorney at any time in connection with the mediation. The Parties understand that each may consult individual counsel of their choosing at any time.

3. **Confidentiality**

a. Scope of Confidentiality. The Parties and the Mediator agree that the entire mediation process is confidential and privileged pursuant to [add reference to statute in your jurisdiction, if there is one]. The Parties and the Mediator agree not to disclose any communications, whether oral or written, made by the Parties in connection with the mediation, except (i) where disclosure is required by law or court rule or (ii) as otherwise provided in this Agreement.

b. Exceptions to Confidentiality
   i. The Parties may disclose information about the mediation to their respective attorneys (if any), therapists (if any), and financial advisors (if any) so long as each such individual is made aware of this confidentiality provision prior to disclosure and agrees to be bound by it.
   ii. The confidentiality provided for in this Agreement shall not preclude disclosure to appropriate authorities of information obtained in the course of the mediation concerning (a) child abuse or neglect, (b) elder abuse or neglect, (c) the risk of serious harm to an individual, or (d) unlawful activity.
   iii. The Mediator may communicate with the EMPLOYER CONTACT regarding general status updates, but those updates shall not include any specific statements made by any of the Parties or information the Parties designate as confidential, unless all Parties agree in writing to a disclosure.

c. Testimony. The Parties agree that they shall not seek to obtain (i) the testimony of another Party or of the Mediator regarding the mediation or (ii) the disclosure of the Mediator's file, and that if either Party seeks such testimony or disclosure by the Mediator in contravention of this provision, that person shall reimburse the Mediator for all costs in connection therewith, including reasonable attorney's fees, and shall compensate the Mediator for time spent, such compensation to be at the Mediator's then-current hourly rate.

d. Separate Meetings. We understand that the Mediator may communicate with each of the Parties separately as part of the mediation process and that, in connection with any such separate communication, a Party may request that the Mediator keep confidential all or part of what was communicated. The Mediator agrees to honor all such requests except to the extent that the substance of the communication falls within one of the exceptions to confidentiality set forth in this Agreement.

e. Stenographic Record. The Parties and the Mediator agree that there shall be no stenographic record or other recording of any meeting, but that the Parties and the Mediator may take notes during the mediation sessions.
f. Video/Audio Record. Unless the Mediator and the Parties agree otherwise in writing in advance, they shall (i) refrain from making a video or audio recording of the mediation session, or streaming the audio or video on the Internet or elsewhere; (ii) keep non-participants from hearing or seeing the mediation when using audio- or video-conferencing for the mediation; and (iii) refrain from using an artificial-intelligence function to generate a summary or transcript of the mediation session.
g. Documents. Any documents exchanged by the Parties in connection with the mediation shall be considered confidential and privileged, provided however that documents that are independently obtained and admissible shall not be rendered confidential or inadmissible because they are produced in connection with the mediation process.
h. Email Communications. Email often plays a large role in the Parties' communications with the Mediator. Please note that if the Parties use email hosted on an employer's server or a shared email account, the ordinary rules concerning privilege may not apply, and therefore the Parties are encouraged to use a private email account for all such communication.
i. Duration of Confidentiality Obligations. The confidentiality obligations set forth in this Agreement shall remain in effect even after the completion of the mediation process, regardless of whether the case is resolved by settlement or not.

4. **Disclosure of Prior Relationships**

   a. The Mediator's Obligation. The Mediator has made a reasonable effort to learn and has disclosed to the Parties (a) all social, business, or professional relationships of which the Mediator is aware that the Mediator and/or the Mediator's firm has had with the Parties; (b) any financial interest the Mediator has in any Party or in the outcome of the case; and

(c) any other circumstances that may create doubt regarding the Mediator's impartiality in the mediation.

b. The Parties' Obligation. The Parties hereby confirm that they are not aware of any conflict of interest with regard to the Mediator's serving in this matter, or any prior relationship with the Mediator or the Mediator's firm that has not been disclosed. The Mediator's resume is available at our website: www.______________.com, and it lists the firms and organizations with which the Mediator has been affiliated; the Parties agree to advise the Mediator as soon as possible if they have any difficulty accessing this document.

5. **Future Relationships**

   a. Neither the Mediator nor the Mediator's firm shall undertake any work for or against a Party regarding the subject matter of the mediation.

   b. The Mediator shall not personally work on any matter for or against a Party, regardless of subject matter, until one year after termination of her services as Mediator.

   c. The Mediator's firm may work on matters for or against either Party if such matters are unrelated to the subject matter of the mediation, provided however that if such work is done, the Mediator shall establish appropriate safeguards to ensure that other members and employees of the Mediator's firm working on any such matter do not have access to any confidential information obtained by the Mediator during the course of the mediation.

6. **Compensation**

   a. Services Covered by This Agreement. EMPLOYER agrees to pay MEDIATOR'S FIRM for the Mediator's time at the hourly rate of $____. The Parties understand that they will be billed for all time spent in preparation for and at mediation sessions, in telephone conferences, for sending and responding to emails, preparing documents, whether before, during, or after the mediation session(s), and review of memos and other material submitted to the Mediator by the Parties.

b. Retainer. EMPLOYER agrees to pay a retainer of $______ at the commencement of the mediation process, which will be applied toward the mediation services rendered. EMPLOYER agrees to replenish the retainer to $______ when the retainer falls below that amount. The retainer will be deposited in a segregated client funds account, and any unused portion of the retainer will be returned to EMPLOYER at the conclusion of the mediation or at such time as the Parties may wish to terminate the mediation. Please note that the retainer is not an estimate of the total cost for your case.

c. Cancellation. In the event that the Parties cancel a scheduled mediation session on less than two weeks' notice to the Mediator, the Mediator will bill a cancellation charge equal to 50 percent of the time charges for the time reserved for the mediation (the "cancellation fee").

d. Billing. MEDIATOR'S FIRM issues bills monthly, normally on or about the 15th of each month, for the work done in the previous month, and payments are due upon receipt of the statement. Bills show the amount of time, in tenths of an hour, spent on the case, as well as costs and expenses. If a bill remains unpaid for more than 30 days after it is sent, MEDIATOR'S FIRM charges interest at the rate of one percent (1%) per month on the unpaid balance starting on the first day of the following month—in other words, approximately 45 days after the bill is sent. (Bills will be sent via email unless the Parties prefer to have them sent by mail.) EMPLOYER agrees that if it has an objection to a bill, it will bring it to MEDIATOR'S FIRM's attention within 60 days from the date that the bill is sent; absent such an objection, the bill will be considered final. Any changes in MEDIATOR'S FIRM's bills or billing arrangements need to be made in writing. In the event of a disagreement about MEDIATOR'S FIRM's charges for fees or expenses, EMPLOYER and MEDIATOR'S FIRM agree to place the matter before the Fee Arbitration Board of the [insert reference to the bar association in your jurisdiction] and agree to be bound by the decision of the arbitrator(s).

7. **Miscellaneous**
   a. Entire Agreement. This Agreement constitutes the entire agreement of the Parties and the Mediator as to the mediation described above and supersedes all previous oral or written agreements between or among them regarding this mediation.
   b. Modification. No modification of this Agreement may be made except in a writing signed by the Parties and the Mediator.
   c. Governing Law. The terms of this Agreement shall be governed by the law of the [insert the name of your jurisdiction] without regard to conflicts of laws or choice of law principles.
   d. Counterparts. This Agreement may be executed in one or more counterparts, each of which shall be deemed an original, and all of which together shall be deemed to be one and the same instrument, and may be executed electronically.

______________________	______________________
PARTY A	PARTY B
Date: ______________________	Date: ______________________
______________________	______________________
Mediator	For EMPLOYER, as to payment obligations in this Agreement
Date: ______________________	Date: ______________________

Appendix C

Sample FAQs About Workplace Mediations

The following set of FAQs might be a useful resource for an internal employer contact (i.e., Human Resources, ombuds, department leader, etc.) in fielding questions from employees considering a workplace mediation as a means to improve a challenging dynamic with a colleague.

What is mediation?
Mediation is a voluntary process in which a neutral third party (the mediator) assists the participants, or parties, in resolving their dispute or conflict by facilitating their discussion.

Can I participate in mediation virtually?
Mediation can be conducted by phone or by videoconference (e.g., via Zoom, etc.), as well as in person.

What is the role of the mediator?
The mediator's role is to help the parties have a more productive conversation to enable them to reach an agreement or shared understanding about how best to move forward. The mediator is not a "decider"—in other words, unlike a judge or an arbitrator, a mediator has no power to impose a resolution on the parties.

What might be an outcome from mediation?
In situations where the parties will continue to have a working relationship, they often emerge from the mediation with a better understanding of each other and/or agreements about how to work more productively together in the future. In some instances, the parties may decide to memorialize their ideas and commitments in writing, to have a shared document to refer back to as they move forward and implement their ideas to improve the working relationship.

Is mediation confidential?
When people enter into a mediation, they sign an Agreement to Mediate in which they agree that the entire mediation process (e.g., pre-mediation conversations with the mediator, conversations with the mediator and with each other during the mediation, and written communications related to the mediation, etc.) is confidential. However, information obtained in the course of the mediation concerning (a) child abuse or neglect, (b) elder abuse or neglect, (c) the risk of serious harm to an individual, or (d) unlawful activity may be disclosed to appropriate authorities.

How long does mediation last?
The mediator and parties will decide at the outset on the duration of the mediation. Depending on the number of topics the participants would like to discuss in mediation, the mediation session may last between 90 minutes and four hours. In some instances, parties are interested in continuing the discussion in a subsequent mediation session. If an additional mediation session is scheduled, the mediator may also offer to meet one-on-one with each party if they would like to "check-in" privately with the mediator to debrief the first session and prepare for the second session as well.

Will the mediator write up our agreement at the end of the mediation?
If the mediation parties are able to reach an agreement or understanding about how to move forward, they will determine what, if anything should be memorialized in writing. While the parties themselves determine what is in the agreement, the mediator can assist them in this process, such as

by serving as a scribe to help summarize their agreements or commitments in a follow-up email to parties.

What happens if a participant fails to do what they said they would do in mediation?

One benefit of mediation is that the participants decide what any mediated agreement will look like. Participants generally follow through on their commitments even when they choose not to put their agreement in writing. For some participants, there is considerable value in the clarity that a written agreement provides. And in some cases, participants may want a signed agreement that is legally enforceable, in which case the participants should get legal advice.

Appendix D

Sample Process Overview for Workplace Mediation Cases

The following process overview could be shared by Human Resources, an employment lawyer, mediator, or ombuds to explain the process to a prospective participant in workplace mediation.

- **Initial 1:1 prep conversation:** The purpose of the one-on-one prep conversation is to allow the mediator to introduce herself, answer any questions about the mediation process, and learn what would be most helpful to discuss in the mediation session. (Duration: 30–60 mins/person)
- **First mediation session:** The mediator and parties meet together (in person or virtually) to begin exploring the topics identified by parties in the one-on-one prep conversations. (Duration: 1.5–2 hours)
- **Follow up 1:1 debrief/prep meeting:** The mediator may typically offer a brief one-on-one debrief/prep conversation (via phone or Zoom) between sessions for any party who would like to connect before the second meeting to debrief the first meeting and/or discuss what would be most helpful to explore in the second meeting. (Duration: 30–60 mins/person)
- **Second mediation session:** This follow-up conversation will continue where things left off in the first session and address anything

new that may have surfaced since then, with the goal of identifying or confirming ideas for how to move forward together. (Duration: 1.5–2 hours)

- **Possible third mediation session:** At times, it is helpful to have a further check-in meeting (perhaps several weeks after the second session) to have a built-in opportunity to discuss what is working well and areas for further discussion in how the parties are working together. (Duration: 1.5–2 hours)

Appendix E

Sample Prep Questions for Workplace Mediation Parties

A subset of the following questions might be shared with mediation parties during a pre-mediation conversation or before the first mediation session as preparatory questions. The questions aim to invite reflection on a party's own experiences as well as to prepare the party to engage and learn from the other person's experience and interests.

Overall Goals

- What might happen in the mediation to make you feel it was a good use of your time?

Discussion Topics

- What topics do you want to explore in mediation? Any subjects you don't want to discuss?
- What might we be able to discuss together to help move things forward?

Exchanging Perspectives

- What's one thing you'd like to learn in this process?
- What's one thing the other person doesn't know now that might be helpful for them to learn—and is something you're open to talking about?

- What is the other person getting wrong about you or your intentions?
- What do you wish they knew about you?

Mediator's Role

- What one thing (or two or three things) can the mediator do to help you participate fully?
- Is there some part of the process, as described by the mediator or in the Agreement to Mediate, that you especially welcome or worry about?

Going Forward

- What does a productive professional partnership or collaboration look like to you?
- With your respective experiences and areas of expertise, what are ways to work together to advance the mission of [EMPLOYER] / support your team's objectives?
- What might be helpful to discuss as possible changes to how you two are working together and communicating?
- How do you prefer to receive information / ideas / suggestions?
- How would you each like to collaborate in your work (i.e., areas for autonomy, input, information sharing, etc.)?
- If you disagree about how to work together in the future, what would you want the other person to do (or not do) to enable you to engage fully in a conversation together?

Appendix F

Newly Promoted: A Workplace Mediation Role Play

The following could be used as a practice opportunity for mediators transitioning into this type of mediation practice, either as a role play or for discussion purposes. If used as a role play, all information could be shared with all role players and the mediator. Or for a more realistic experience, the individual information (i.e., "Mateo's Perspective" and "Letitia's Perspective") could be distributed to that role-playing party only (i.e., the role player for Mateo receives only "Mateo's Perspective," and the role player for Letitia receives only "Letitia's Perspective"), and the mediator role player could receive only the general background information.

Background

Mateo and Letitia have been colleagues in the same City of Ames office for the past four years. In that time, the two have worked closely together on a number of projects under the supervision of Tyler, a longtime employee. They occasionally socialized outside the office, taking lunch breaks together or grabbing a drink at a nearby bar's happy hour on the way home. By all accounts, the two had a collaborative working relationship.

Six months ago, after Tyler announced his retirement, both Letitia and Mateo applied for the position. Mateo was offered the job and began in the new role three months ago. Since then, the working relationship has become rocky. Mateo has complained that Letitia is unresponsive, lacks attention to detail, and is at times insubordinate (refusing to comply with Mateo's meeting requests or preferred methods of receiving status updates on projects). On the other hand, Letitia has complained that Mateo is a micro-manager who flaunts his "power" whenever possible and does not acknowledge the experience and expertise Letitia brings to the role (Letitia worked at another city office before beginning work in the office at the same time as Mateo).

At this point, both Letitia and Mateo have spoken individually to an HR manager to complain about the current working relationship. After considerable efforts to coach them separately did not help, both agreed to attend a mediation session led by an external mediator.

Mateo's perspective

Mateo believes that Letitia is acting out because she cannot accept that Mateo was selected for the manager position. The two had a great working relationship before—what else could explain this sudden turn in behavior? To make matters worse, when Mateo has tried to give some constructive feedback to Letitia, Letitia has been incredibly defensive, almost hostile. Mateo is thinking of filing a bullying complaint against Letitia, in the hopes of perhaps having someone else in the office take over supervisory responsibility. This would not be ideal but could work, as Letitia often collaborates with a few others in the office. Mateo also misses the collaborative and friendly working relationship that made it fun to be in the office and work the long hours together.

Letitia's perspective

Letitia is frustrated to suddenly have a micro-manager as a boss—and very disappointed that she was not offered the manager position. Tyler trusted Letitia to do the work—why is Mateo so demanding? Letitia thinks that the promotion has gone to Mateo's head and that Letitia should not bear the brunt of things. Letitia has heard that Mateo is considering a bullying complaint, which sounds ridiculous. First, Mateo is the manager, right?

Second, Letitia acknowledges things have gotten heated at times, but in Letitia's family, everyone values debate and direct engagement—doing that shows you care! Letitia doesn't want to change her ways, but she realizes that the current dynamic is not sustainable.

Appendix G

Additional Resources for Mediators

Here are a few resources and institutions I consult to stay current on mediation topics. Although some are not specific to workplace conflicts or mediation, I have found their content engaging and applicable to the workplace context.

- **Program on Negotiation at Harvard Law School (PON):** PON is a clearinghouse for dispute resolution teaching and education. In addition to live and virtual mediation and negotiation programs, PON also has a free virtual series, PON Live!, featuring expert talks on a range of topics. Past sessions are also archived and accessible on the PON website, https://www.pon.harvard.edu/.
- **The Association for Conflict Resolution (ACR):** ACR, which has local chapters in many states and regions, provides opportunities for continuing education and networking with other mediators. The Greater New York chapter has an active online continuing education program that is free and archived on its website, https://www.acrgny.org/.
- **Mediate.com:** This website provides articles, podcasts, and videos on topics ranging from starting your mediation practice to incorporating AI in mediations. Sign up to receive a free weekly e-newsletter to be informed on the topics of the day or visit the site to access past recorded content.

In addition to the sources included in the Bibliography, the following resources may be useful for more in-depth exploration of addressing workplace conflict directly or mediation more generally.

- Fowler, Clare. *Rising Above Office Conflict: A Light-Hearted Guide for the Heavy-Hearted Employee*. Rowman & Littlefield, 2023.
- Gallo, Amy. *Getting Along: How to Work with Anyone (Even Difficult People)*. Harvard Business Review Press, 2022.
- Hoffman, David A. *Mediation: A Practice Guide for Mediators, Lawyers, and Other Professionals*. Massachusetts Continuing Legal Education, 2013.
- Lempereur, Alain, Jacques Salzer, Aurelien Colson, Michele Pekar, and Eugene B. Kogan. *Mediation: Negotiation by Other Moves*. Wiley, 2021.

ACKNOWLEDGMENTS

I have many people to thank for their support and invaluable assistance in bringing this book to fruition.

I am grateful to several wonderful colleagues who were always available to discuss ideas and whose feedback improved the depth, quality, and accessibility of the book. Thank you to David Hoffman for mentorship over the years and thoughtful feedback that has made this book a better resource; I continue to learn from you in our work together in the classroom and in the field. Loraine Della Porta provided insightful suggestions and clarifications at all stages of the project based on her wealth of experience mediating workplace and organizational conflicts. Mike Cohen was an early supporter of the idea and brought a keen eye to his review of multiple drafts, drawing upon his experience in HR and mediation. I am grateful to Marcus Stergio for countless conversations about workplace mediation cases over the years and for his insightful, practitioner-oriented feedback on earlier drafts. I am also thankful to Esther Lin, Amber Garcia-Gonzalez, and Charlotte Hamm for providing thoughtful feedback from their dual areas of expertise in mediation and the ombuds, human resources, and psychology fields, respectively.

I am thankful for the best professional home and family I could have asked for at Boston Law Collaborative, LLC. Thank you to Tracy Bekerian, Jenna Goodman, Jim Grumbach, David Hoffman, Michele Keratsis, Karen Richards, and Lucera Story for continuous support and encouragement throughout my years at BLC.

The Mediation Group has provided additional opportunities for me to mediate workplace cases and learn from insightful colleagues. I am particularly thankful to Brad Honoroff, Jane Honoroff, Amy Gordon, and David Matz for their mentorship and opportunities to debrief cases together over the years.

From my law school days to the present, I am grateful to Sheila Heen, Dan Shapiro, and Doug Stone for enduring mentorship and encouragement. For providing opportunities to teach and experiment, I thank Nicole Bryant and Guhan Subramanian at the Program on Negotiation at Harvard Law School. Thanks also to the entire team at PON, and especially the HMI team headed by Ruth Collins, Lindsay Sullivan, Riley Scheuritzel, and Heather McDonald for their thoughtful and fun collaboration in teaching mediation programs, where I've had the chance to clarify some of my thinking on workplace mediations. A special thanks to Ruth Collins, who was always ready with a word of encouragement and wise, practical advice for writing and teaching.

I was first introduced to mediation as a student in the Harvard Mediation Program and continue to admire its work as a leader in the community mediation space. Thank you to Prill Ellis, Maureen (Mo) Griffin, Cathy Mondell, and Ana Carolina Riella for opportunities to reflect on the challenges mediations present and how mediators might respond.

My work has been deeply impacted by my learning about dialogue from Essential Partners. A special thanks to John Sarrouf, Meg Griffiths, and Nadiya Brock for always extending opportunities for me to learn and find my feet as a dialogue facilitator and supporting my thinking about how to bring this learning into mediation.

People often remark on how the mediation and conflict management field is unique in having a disproportionately high number of thoughtful, giving, and supportive members, and I have been lucky to find such colleagues over the years. I am especially grateful to Brian Blancke, Izzy Brill-Cass, Hon. Beth Butler (ret.), Stevenson Carlebach, Alyson Carrel, Lynn Cohn, Diana Chiang Cooke, Andrew Cornell, Nick Diehl, Mooly Dinnar, Chuck Doran, Katheryn Dutenhaver, Morgan Michele Franklin, Jeff Fraser, Don Greenstein, Josh Hoch, Margaret Huang, Thilo Kerkhoff, Alain Lempereur, Brian Mandell, Liz Marcus, Kylie Millbern, Bob Mnookin, Susan Podziba, Noemi Razso, Joel Reck, Hon. David Sacks (ret.), Gabriella Salvatore, Stephan Sonnenberg, Katy Sullivan, Larry Susskind, Matt Thompson, and Katherine Triantafillou for thoughtful conversations over the years that have enhanced my learning as a mediator and for their camaraderie as mediators. Thank you to Clare Fowler, Grande Lum, Art Hinshaw, Andrea Schneider, Jill DeTemple, Dwight Golann, Forrest "Woody" Mosten, Peter Adler, and Zick Rubin, who each provided invaluable support in the early stages of the book. For reigniting my strong interest in employment and workplace issues, I am thankful to Becky Shuster and Shirley Lee for their mentorship at the MA Commission Against Discrimination.

During the writing of this book, I had the good fortune to be invited to lead a BLC team to provide a series of workplace mediation trainings for City of Boston HR leaders. In working with them, I gained a clearer sense of the challenges and realities of addressing workplace conflicts on the ground as they initially present. I am grateful to the leadership team of Andrea Hennelly, Amber Garcia-Gonzalez, Mariella Collins, and Morgan Cowie-Haskell for their partnership and for bringing me in to understand more deeply when and how mediation may be a helpful intervention.

I am deeply indebted to my wonderful editor, Louisa Williams, who brought the words to life. Thank you for contributing both your editing and mediation expertise, making the process so fun, and bringing clarity to this project. Thank you also to the ABA Publishing team, led by Carlie Wall, for skillfully guiding me through this process. I am grateful to Caryn Shelton-May, the Harvard Law School librarians, and Connor Nickson for excellent research assistance.

I am thankful for a circle of friends who have rooted for me along the way. Special thanks to Rachel Milner Gillers for always being available to talk through ideas and concerns together and Susie Ma for thoughtful feedback and support from start to finish. And a huge thanks to my running group for keeping me on track, whether on the running path or in writing—Deb Becker, Anna Hughes, Yun-kyung Jee, Sara Lopez-Pintado, Danielle Rabina, and Lex Thomas. I am also grateful for friendships that have endured for decades. Thank you to Ariel Green, Chana Schoenberger Zimmerman, Cheryl Gray, Lisa Mahle, Nienke Grossman, Trisha Ball, Geertrui Spaepen, and Shaheen Zojwalla for being there through life's ups and downs. Thank you also to Colleen Suhanosky and Bobby Mendoza for providing a home away from home at Rifrullo, where I enjoyed many conversations with colleagues about this project.

Finally, thank you to Joel, Jasper, and Max for making me laugh, cheering me on with unconditional support, and reminding me what's important.

A NOTE ON RELEVANT ORGANIZATIONS

Boston Law Collaborative, LLC

Boston Law Collaborative, LLC (BLC) is a multidisciplinary law firm devoted to conflict resolution and the practice of collaborative law. BLC team members provide mediation, arbitration, and litigation services, as well as a variety of other services in the role of impartial dispute resolvers. BLC also provides training in all areas of dispute resolution through its Institute. For more information, visit www.blc.law.

Program on Negotiation at Harvard Law School

The Program on Negotiation (PON) is a university consortium dedicated to developing the theory and practice of negotiation, mediation, and dispute resolution. As a community of scholars and practitioners, PON serves a unique role in the world negotiation community. Founded in 1983 as a special research project at Harvard Law School, PON includes faculty, students, and staff from Harvard University, Massachusetts Institute of Technology, and Tufts University. For more information, and to learn more about PON's executive education offerings in mediation, visit https://www.pon.harvard.edu/.

Essential Partners

Founded in 1989, Essential Partners (EP) helps people build relationships across differences to address their communities' most pressing challenges. EP's proven approach helps people live, work, worship, and learn better together. Through richer, healthier, more inclusive communication, people strengthen relationships while gaining new insight into themselves and each other, as well as the problems they face together. For more information, visit whatisessential.org.

BIBLIOGRAPHY

Ahn, Woo-Kyoung. *Thinking 101: How to Reason Better to Live Better.* Flatiron Books, 2023.

American Arbitration Association, American Bar Association, and Association for Conflict Resolution. "Model Standards of Conduct for Mediators." https://www.americanbar.org/content/dam/aba/administrative/dispute_resolution/dispute_resolution/model_standards_conduct_april2007.pdf.

American Bar Association Standing Committee on Ethics and Professional Responsibility, Formal Opinion 518 (2025). "A Lawyer's Duties to Avoid Misleading Communications When Acting as a Third-Party Neutral Mediator." https://www.americanbar.org/content/dam/aba/administrative/professional_responsibility/ethics-opinions/aba-formal-opinion-518.pdf.

Amsler, Lisa Blomgren, Alexander B. Avtgis, and M. Scott Jackman. "Dispute System Design and Bias in Dispute Resolution." *Southern Methodist University Law Review* 70, no. 4 (2017): 913–941.

Argyris, Chris. *Overcoming Organizational Defenses.* Allyn and Bacon, 1990.

Banaji, Mahzarin R., and Anthony G. Greenwald. *Blindspot: Hidden Biases of Good People.* Bantam, 2013.

Bollen, Katalien, and Martin Euwema. "Workplace Mediation: An Underdeveloped Research Area." *Negotiation Journal* 29, no. 3 (2013): 329–353.

Bollen, Katalien, Martin Euwema, and Patrick Müller. "Why Are Subordinates Less Satisfied with Mediation? The Role of Uncertainty." *Negotiation Journal* 26, no. 4 (2010): 417–433.

Bowling, Daniel, and David Hoffman. *Bringing Peace into the Room: How the Personal Qualities of the Mediator Impact the Process of Conflict Resolution.* Jossey-Bass, 2003.

Charkoudian, Lorig, and Ellen Kabcenell Wayne, "Fairness, Understanding, and Satisfaction: Impact of Mediator and Participant Race and Gender on Participants' Perception of Mediation." *Conflict Resolution Quarterly* 8, no. 1 (2010): 23–52.

Cloke, Ken. *Mediating Dangerously.* Jossey-Bass, 2001.

Cloke, Ken, and Joan Goldsmith. *Resolving Conflicts at Work.* Jossey-Bass, 2000.

Davis, Wayne. "The Circle Chart: A Tool for Organized Thinking." Harvard Negotiation Project (February 13, 2024). https://www.pon.harvard.edu/wp-content/uploads/images/posts/The-Circle-Chart.pdf.

Della Porta, Loraine. "Do You Need an Organizational Climate Assessment?" The Mediation Group (May 23, 2023). https://www.themediationgroup.org/blog-posts/do-you-need-an-organizational-climate-assessment.

DeTemple, Jill. "The Spaces We Make: Dialogic Classrooms and Social Transformation." *Ohio State Journal on Dispute Resolution* 35, no. 5 (2020): 753–780.

DeTemple, Jill, Harriett E. Hayes, and Jennifer Ellis West. "When Students Listen to Themselves: Reflection as Critical Practice." In *The Dialogic Classroom in Higher Education: Revolutionary Listening for Curiosity, Engagement, and Deep Learning.* Routledge, 2026.

Essential Partners. "Sample Connecting Questions" (June 5, 2020). https://whatisessential.org/resources/Sample-connecting-questions-0.

Fisher, Roger, William Ury, and Bruce Patton. *Getting to Yes.* 2nd ed. Penguin Putnam, 2006.

Fisher, Roger, and Daniel Shapiro. *Beyond Reason: Using Emotions as You Negotiate.* Penguin, 2005.

Folger, Joseph, and Robert A. Baruch Bush. "Transformative Mediation." *International Journal of Conflict Engagement and Resolution* 2, no. 1 (2014): 20–34.

Friedman, Gary, and Jack Himmelstein. *Challenging Conflict: Mediation Through Understanding.* American Bar Association, 2009.

Galton, Eric. *Ripples from Peace Lake: Essays for Mediators and Peacemakers.* Trafford, 2006.

Galton, Eric. "A Blunder." In *Stories Mediators Tell*, edited by Eric Galton and Lela P. Love. American Bar Association, 2012.

Golann, Dwight. "'I Sometimes Catch Myself Looking Angry or Tired . . .': The Impact of Mediating by Zoom." *Alternatives to the High Cost of Litigation* 39, no. 5 (2021): 73–86.

Griffiths, Meg, Betsy Hayes, and Audrey Lee. "The Dialogic Classroom." PowerPoint presentation for The Dialogic Classroom. Essential Partners. June 4–5, 2025.

Hoffman, David A. "Mediation and the Art of Shuttle Diplomacy." *Negotiation Journal* 27, no. 3 (2011): 263–309.

Hoffman, David A. "Confidentiality, Privilege and Other Legal Issues in Mediation" and "Enforceability of Agreements." In *Mediation: A Practice Guide for Mediators, Lawyers, and Other Professionals.* Massachusetts Continuing Legal Education, 2013.

Hoffman, David A., and Helen Winter. "Follow the Science: Proven Strategies for Reducing Unconscious Bias." *Harvard Negotiation Law Review* 8, no. 1 (2022): 1–63.

Izumi, Carol. "Implicit Bias and the Illusion of Mediator Neutrality." *Washington University Journal of Law and Policy* 34 (2010).

Kahneman, Daniel. *Thinking, Fast and Slow*. Farrar, Straus and Giroux, 2011.

Kalter, Meriem, Katalien Bollen, Martin Euwema, and Alain-Laurent Verbeke. "A Matter of Feelings: Mediators' Perceptions of Emotions in Hierarchical Workplace Conflicts." *Frontiers in Psychology* 12 (2021): 1–13.

Kalter, Meriem, Katalien Bollen, and Martin Euwema. "The Long-Term Effectiveness of Mediating Workplace Conflicts." *Negotiation Journal* 34, no. 3 (2018): 243–264.

Krockow, Eva. "The Halo Effect: What It Is and How to Beat It." *Psychology Today*, October 8, 2021. https://www.psychologytoday.com/us/blog/stretching-theory/202110/the-halo-effect-what-it-is-and-how-beat-it.

Lee, Audrey J. "Working with Emotional Interests in Mediation." *American Bar Association Dispute Resolution Magazine* 31, no. 2 (2025): 29–31.

Lee, Audrey J. "Mediating Conflicts at Work: Post-COVID Shifts in Resolving Employment Disputes." *Massachusetts Bar Association Section Review* (2023): 7–8.

Lee, Audrey J. "Implicit Bias in Mediation," *Harvard Negotiation Law Review* 25, no. 2 (2020): 167–186.

Malhotra, Ruchika T. "How to Reduce Personal Bias When Hiring." *Harvard Business Review*, June 28, 2019. https://hbr.org/2019/06/how-to-reduce-personal-bias-when-hiring.

McDermott, Patrick, and Ruth Obar. "The Equal Employment Opportunity Commission Mediation Participants Experience in Online Mediation and Comparison to In-Person Mediation," February 18, 2022. https://www.eeoc.gov/equal-employment-opportunity-commission-mediators-perception-remote-mediation-and-comparisons.

Mediate.com. "Connecticut to Become Thirteenth State to Adopt Uniform Mediation Act on October 1, 2025," September 24, 2025. https://mediate.com/news/connecticut-to-become-thirteenth-state-to-adopt-uniform-mediation-act-on-october-1-2025/.

National Labor Relations Board. "Weingarten Rights." Accessed November 23, 2025. https://www.nlrb.gov/about-nlrb/rights-we-protect/your-rights/weingarten-rights.

Press, Sharon, and Paul M. Lurie. "A Mediator's Obligation to Memorialize the Agreement." *American Bar Association Dispute Resolution Magazine* (2015): 39–41.

Riskin, Leonard L. "A Conversation with Professor Leonard Riskin About Mindfulness, Dispute Resolution, and Mindfulness Resources for Mediators." Interview by Linda Lazarus. www.mediate.com, February 22, 2005. https://mediate.com/a-conversation-with-professor-leonard-riskin-about-mindfulness-dispute-resolution-and-mindfulness-resources-for-mediators/.

Riskin, Leonard L. "Decision-Making in Mediation: The New Old Grid and the New New Grid System." *Notre Dame Law Review* 79, no. 1 (2003): 1–53.

Robbennolt, Jennifer K., and Jean R. Sternlight. *Psychology for Lawyers*. 2nd ed. American Bar Association, 2021.

Sarrouf, John. "In Pursuit of the Dialogic Classroom: Designing Spaces for Conviction." In *Bias, Belief, and Conviction in an Age of Fake Facts*. Routledge, 2022.

Shaw, Margaret. "Random Conversation." In *Stories Mediators Tell*, edited by Eric R. Galton and Lela P. Love. American Bar Association, 2012.

Stains, Jr., Robert R. "Reflection for Connection: Deepening Dialogue Through Reflective Processes." *Conflict Resolution Quarterly* 30, no. 1 (2012): 33–51.

Stone, Douglas, Sheila Heen, and Bruce Patton. *Difficult Conversations: How to Discuss What Matters Most*. 3rd ed. Penguin Books, 2023.

Swaab, Roderick I. "Face First: Pre-Mediation Caucus and Face in Employment Disputes." Paper presented at the 22nd Annual International Association of Conflict Management Conference, Kyoto, Japan, June 15, 2009, http://dx.doi.org/10.2139/ssrn.1493514.

Wissler, Roselle, and Art Hinshaw. "The Role Different Factors Play in the Use of Initial Joint Sessions or Initial Caucuses." *American Bar Association Dispute Resolution Magazine* (2025). https://www.americanbar.org/groups/dispute_resolution/resources/magazine/2025-april/role-factors-play-initial-joint-sessions-caucuses/.

INDEX